REBEL WITCH

ABOUT THE AUTHOR

Kelly-Ann Maddox was made in Merseyside, England, in the 1980s under a Sagittarius sun with a shock of black hair and a face like the full moon. As a kid, she checked inside wardrobes to see if Narnia was back there somewhere. Before realizing that she was a real witch, she would often pretend to be one, quoting from the witches of Disney films, mixing potions with the bath-water bubbles and donning her nana's costume jewellery to create the perfect look of an empowered enchantress.

As she started her serious reading in her teens, she understood that she was stepping into witchhood for real. In fact, being a witch was often the singular point of strength and inspiration that got her through the toughest times during the ongoing mental health issues she endured for years. Knowing how much her practice of the craft nurtured and supported her through those difficult times, she began creating online resources in her 20s, to help other people explore the path in an individualized way.

Kelly-Ann now lives alone in Kent, UK. She is an award-winning professional Tarot reader, Tarot teacher and certified spiritual counsellor, helping clients all over the world with her readings, sessions and mentoring. She has created hundreds of YouTube videos to inspire her viewers to take charge of their lives and be freewheeling spiritual beings.

Kelly-Ann is also a collage artist and poet. She is a committed vegan.

You can contact Kelly-Ann here:

mail@kelly-annmaddox.com

Kelly-Ann Maddox
PO Box
83 Ducie Street
Manchester
M1 2JQ

REBEL WITCH

Carve the Craft that's Yours Alone

Kelly-Ann Maddox

WATKINS
Sharing Wisdom Since 1893

This edition first published in the UK and USA in 2021 by
Watkins, an imprint of Watkins Media Limited
Unit 11, Shepperton House
89–93 Shepperton Road
London N1 3DF

enquiries@watkinspublishing.com

10 9 8 7 6 5 4 3 2 1

Designed by Francesca Corsini

Typeset by JCS Publishing Services Ltd

Printed and bound in the UK by TJ Books Limited

A CIP record for this book is available from the British Library.

ISBN: 978-1-78678-427-8 (Hardback)

ISBN: 978-1-78678-468-1 (eBook)

www.watkinspublishing.com

For Dani, without whom none of me would be possible.

We're just two badgers in search of acorns.

ACKNOWLEDGEMENTS

Thank you so much to Fiona Robertson at Watkins for understanding exactly what I wanted to write and bringing some order to the chaos. You were the long-suffering midwife that I needed to help me birth this book. I had no idea that I would go through so much in my personal life whilst writing *Rebel Witch* and you were kind and encouraging when I found the process tough for that reason. I also appreciate everyone at Watkins who helped bring this book to life. I hope you're happy with the result.

Thank you to Ethony Dawn for making the introduction. When you put Fiona in touch with me, you performed a magickal act and I deeply appreciate it.

Thank you to Jenny Lloyd for your visionary illustrations and for your friendship. Your work has done so much for the book, just as you have done so much for me as a human being.

Thanks to so many of my loved ones who believed in me, checked in on me during the writing process and offered distraction and conversation when I needed it. If you talked with me, walked with me, asked me how things were going or kept connected to me during the two lockdowns I experienced whilst working on the book, I appreciate you. A special thank you to those who were there when I was really low. You know who you are.

Thank you to every member of my online community who has subscribed to my channel, commented on my videos, followed me on social media and been invested in my message over the course of time. To the witchcraft and cardslinger communities on YouTube, thank you for the creativity and dialogue over the years.

To every single one of my clients and Patreon members, a massive thank you. Your financial and emotional investment in my work is one of the greatest gifts in my life.

Thank you to my mum – a practitioner of sacred rebellion. Your cycle-breaking led me here.

CONTENTS

WHY THIS BOOK
EXISTS AND
HOW TO USE IT

Hey there, cherry pie! I'm thrilled to be strapping myself into this weird witchy ride with you and I want to start by letting you know why this book was born and how I'm hoping that it can serve you.

First, let me level with you. There's no shortage of books out there to give you the bare bones of a decent solitary witchcraft practice. In fact, there's a shit-ton of them. Those books help you to understand the common concepts, activities and tools utilized by witchy types to improve life and get desired results. *Rebel Witch* contains a lot of that same information too, but that's not why it was written.

Instead, it's intended as a tool for sparking inspiration. It's an invitation to build a practice that looks, sounds and feels like your very own psyche – a practice that reflects your authentic experiences, memories and personality traits so much that it's undeniably *your* unique living tradition.

The building blocks of the craft *are* offered within the pages of this book. We'll certainly cover things like creating sacred space, choosing and using tools, working with deities and casting spells. But, together, we'll also discover ways to mould these elements of the craft into *your* particular shape. This book will invite you to decide how things might need some tweaking and tailoring to suit your individual needs. It will empower you to decide what really makes your heart do the witchy fandango! It will encourage you to swerve the stuff that doesn't feel genuinely relevant to you, leave behind what doesn't resonate and boldly invent your own tradition. If advice on how to be a witch doesn't quite hit the spot or feels a bit dusty or boring, why follow it?! *Rebel Witch* is intended to champion sovereignty and identity, so you're never stuck for ideas about how to make your path more authentic. I've made lists of ideas for you to try out, but they're not intended to be used as rigid instructions. Instead, I hope they help you to extend your sense of what's possible.

The other thing I've strived to achieve with *Rebel Witch* is as much of a sense of inclusion as possible. Witches are so varied in their experiences, lifestyles, preferences and capabilities, and I've tried to be mindful of that. I've avoided giving advice like, "Physical movement is the best way to raise energy for magick", which is kind of like telling those who can't move around much due to pain, injury or other circumstances that they're missing out on the top-shelf energy-raising stuff. It simply isn't fair or true to state that you need movement to get to the height of energetic potency. It's possible to raise energy for magick without moving a muscle! So I've always tried to give a wide range of suggestions so there'll be something to suit the kind of witchcraft you'll be doing. I've tried to be expansive, not narrow – imaginative rather than strict! Some witchy resources insist that handwriting is the only way to record your experiences in witchcraft or that you need to write spells and intentions "pen to paper", presuming that this is somehow more legitimate than typing into a phone, computer or tablet. But why should handwritten records be more legit or meaningful? Why should we decide that those who don't like to write by hand are essentially doing a lesser and weaker version of magickal recordkeeping? Who came up with the notion that witches can't type records, voice-dictate them or just do away with keeping them at all if they don't seem helpful? I want *Rebel Witch* to help you figure out what your way is. Some resources overly stress the importance of prolonged concentration as a critical form of witchy brain training. For instance, I've seen it suggested that a witch should be able to do long meditations or focus on a candle flame for extended periods and whatnot. This may not be possible for someone with ADHD and nor is it tenable for someone with two kids under five. You get the picture. *Rebel Witch* does not presume that you are like me, or like anyone else. It invites you to be your own resplendent witchy self. Of course, I know I'm not going to get it completely right. There's often room for improvement when it comes to inclusion and it's hard not to see life through one's own lens. But I hope you'll find plenty of things to resonate with, whoever you are and whatever shape your life is taking.

I've tried to avoid including language and concepts from specific cultural practices that I'm not involved in. I acknowledge that some of the ideas fostered in the witchcraft world have their roots in marginalized communities and have sometimes been extracted from a much more complex structure of belief. Some ideas have been simplified and commodified with no recognition given to the cultures from which they originated. For this reason, I've avoided using terms such as "smudging" and "spirit animal", and I'm not going to be talking you through the chakra system. I see no issue with learning about ideas and practices from all over the world, but I want to avoid poorly explaining a powerful concept from outside my own cultural understanding and then encouraging other witches to take that half-baked explanation and run with it. As you design and refine your personalized practice, you can include ideas that honour your cultural identity and heritage. I trust that you can figure out for yourself what's appropriate. My aim is to ensure that I'm not extracting stuff randomly from its roots and presenting it to you in an irresponsible or insensitive way.

How to Navigate this Book

The book is served up as three tasty courses, by the end of which I hope you'll be feeling well fed. In Part I, we'll look at the meaning of the word "witch" and how you want that meaning to roll out in your life. I'll encourage you to decide on your aims and consider how much you want to expose your path to others. This first part also sets the tone for the rest of the book, reminding you that it's all about creating a practice that honours your individuality rather than following instructions and suggestions to the letter. Part II is all about taking action. We'll examine how to work with energy, connect with non-human beings and set up altars, how to cast spells and do rituals and divination – and so much more. The rubber meets the road here – it's all about what you'll actually be doing in your craft. Part III sends you off on your journey, with advice about ethics, creating an inspiring schedule for your practice and troubleshooting problems as they arise. I want to make sure you feel as confident as possible in your practice when we finally part ways, so in these pages I'll be tying up loose ends and giving helpful reminders.

At the start of Part I, Part II and Part III, you'll find a talisman that symbolizes the aim of that particular section of the book. Each talisman can be used as a visual reminder of the intention behind the work we're doing in each stage. Gaze at the talismans as you fuel yourself with excitement, discipline and determination. Use the words of power that are offered with each image, repeating them aloud or in your head before you start to read each part of the book and again when you reach its end. You could scan and print the talismans to place on your altar or in a book you may be using to record your progress. Take the talismans as far as you want. They are offered to inspire you and to remind you of the significance and beauty of the rebel witch journey that you are taking.

At the end of each segment, I've offered suggestions for solo activities so that you can deep-dive in your own sacred time. There are two categories of activity: "Write it" and "Try it".

"Write it" offers prompts for journaling, notetaking and brainstorming sessions. If you're all about writing stuff down, then you might want to decide where you're going to be keeping your rebel witch written exercises as you go along. You might choose to pop them into an existing witchy book where you're already recording your thoughts, or you may feel that a new book is required. (It really doesn't have to be fancy and can, of course, be made of recycled paper and from a sustainable source.) Maybe you'll just do the writing on loose-leaf paper. If you don't like to handwrite, you can absolutely type your writing exercises and keep them on your phone, laptop, tablet or PC. Or you may want to record spoken responses using audio notes on your phone. Whatever works best. You might, for any number of reasons, be the type who dislikes *keeping* your written thoughts, so feel free to delete digital records when the time is right, or shred paper up for recycling once you feel you've extracted the necessary juice from the exercise. Burning paper in your cauldron or on an open fire may also work for you.

"Try it" offers practical exercises and suggestions for actions. Sometimes the prompts will be mindset shifts to try throughout your day. Sometimes they will urge you to do some research, change up your routine or try a visualization or ritual. You can customize these suggestions to make them more suitable for you. They are intended to inspire and motivate. So, if you can see a way of tweaking a suggested action so that it makes you feel more fizzy, be my guest. If you're really not feeling a prompt, by all means skip it. You might decide to try other stuff instead, because it's more relevant or more challenging for you. Fair play – go for it!

You get to choose how much involvement you need in each topic. You might not choose to complete each exercise. There are some you may relish and devour, while others you may skip over and come back to in the future. You can take what resonates and absolutely leave the rest. *Rebel Witch* does not seek to bully or dictate. It's intended to work like a skeleton key, opening lots of doors for you but always placing the power to choose in your own hands. Don't let me – or anyone else – tell you what to do. My hope is that by the end of this book you will feel liberated, empowered and excited to be carrying on carving the craft that's uniquely yours.

Let's get weird, dollface.

Statement of Power: *From the high clouds of my imagination, my path flows and weaves. It is unique to me. As it shines, grows and stretches on into my future, I know that its roots lie in the depths of my unique beingness.*

Part I
LET'S BEGIN

Part I is designed to help you lay some foundations for your uniquely designed path. I'll introduce you to the concept of a rebel witch, welcoming you to celebrate the value of going your own way in witchcraft while also inviting you to think about the challenges you may encounter. You'll have a chance to figure out how much you want to reveal your witchy world to others and what your true aims as a witch will be. Let's dive in ...

WHAT DOES "WITCH" REALLY MEAN?

There's never a dull moment with the word "witch"! It provokes all kinds of reactions, doesn't it? For some people, it's a word surrounded by fear and fuelled by anxiety. For others, it invokes fantasy and fairy tale. For many, it does both. Of course, the word "witch" *is* associated with both reality and make-believe. The warty, cackling, child-snatching kind of witch isn't what we're focusing on here, though it does deliver delicious imagery and make for great stories. These days, though, "witch" has been thoroughly reclaimed to describe people with a specific set of spiritual leanings, who engage in spellcraft and other glorious magickal practices. And that's the type we're on about here. To countless people in the modern world (including me), a witch is essentially someone who believes they have some degree of mystical power over events and outcomes that goes beyond the causality acknowledged by modern science.

"Witch" comes from the Old English word for practitioners of witchcraft: *wicce* was used to describe female witches and *wicca* for male. This later turned into the Middle English *wicche*, which described practitioners regardless of gender. Throughout history, witches and those falsely believed to be witches have been heinously persecuted. Witch trials resulting in hangings, drownings and burnings were carried out in the name of Christianity, and in the further reading list (see pages 251–2), I have directed you to some amazing books to help you learn more about this if you wish. It would be wrong to suggest that witches don't deal with discrimination in the modern world because many absolutely do. It can still be risky to identify outwardly as a witch and, unfortunately, in some cultures it can still result in social isolation, violence and death. Again, the suggested reading list will direct you to some material to help you understand more about this ongoing issue.

Plenty of peeps would say that witches wield personal power through the magickal pursuit of their desires. Through their spells and other activities, they banish, heal and flourish. Others emphasize that a witch honours the cycles of nature, maintains the sacred traditions of the land and brings healing to the planet. Witches do use their power in different ways and while some witchy paths look incredibly similar, others diverge wildly. But most witches agree that their objective is to pursue their needs and desires, and those of their communities, using spells, rituals and other spiritual formulae to direct energy *toward* a certain set of results or *away* from other, undesired ones. Witches seek control over their reality through spiritual practices and those practices are usually repeated on a regular basis, even if they change over time.

For most, "witch" can also be understood as a verb. Witches are practitioners. They walk their talk. If you wanted to, you could fancy yourself as a witch and just *say* you are without taking action. However, you probably wouldn't feel right using the word to describe yourself because you'd sense that being a witch is more than just a way of seeing the world – it's also a way of living in it. In order for a witch to be true to themselves, they've got to be moving and shaking! Witches build up their skills, they dabble, they experiment and they often specialize. While it's common for witches to be bookish (though this is not a requirement at all), *to witch* is to walk the path by living it, rather than just learning how it could be lived. This book will help you figure out how to do that in your own exclusive way. Your path is a one-off, honey bee! It's going to be as potent as possible for you as an individual. Of course, if you just want to

WHAT DOES "WITCH" REALLY MEAN?

say you're a witch without changing anything in your life or taking any witchy actions, I mean, fine. No one can stop a person from doing that, but it seems fruitless. And as you're reading these words right now, I know you're not someone who wants to stand on the sidelines wearing the label without doing the work!

What's your personal history with this powerful, hard-hitting word? Maybe you've been claiming "witch" to describe yourself for years and feel only positive things about it, or maybe you've been growing curious and find the word tantalizing and exciting. But if "witch" has more negative associations for you, don't worry. Many people find themselves re-evaluating the word at some point. Someone who comes from a religious household where "witch" was associated with wrongdoing and evil will need to untangle it from that web of judgements. Likewise, if you only ever thought of witches as crooked-nosed women who cackled and ate babies, you will need to allow yourself to grasp its real-world definition rather than just thinking in terms of fantasy beings.

What a Witch Does

A common misconception is that witches defy the laws of science and therefore could never exist in reality. But actually, witches tend to respect and pursue scientific knowledge. They just also appreciate that there is so much that's not fully understood in terms of Western science and that their experiences on the magickal journey are undeniably profound. Most witches you come across don't see themselves as being able to defy science by moving things without touching them, for instance. They're more likely to feel that they complement scientific reality with a keen appreciation for evidence gathered beyond the bounds of mainstream research. Witches are scientists themselves – scientists of a mystical variety. They record patterns that occur in their practices and they tweak their witchcraft to get better results. They find powerful ways of making things happen, both internally (in their psychology) and externally (in their experiences and environments). Just because witches are often working with ideas that are not widely accepted by the scientific community doesn't mean that they are anti-science. They just also believe in the weird stuff that seems to defy scientific explanation sometimes.

A witchy practice usually includes rituals, spells and celebration of the natural cycles of Earth among other things. When it comes to spells, it's worth pointing out that some witches do more actual spellcraft than others. For many, it's ritual and divination, rather than spells, that are the favoured activities (and we'll get into what all these terms mean as we go through the book together). Some practitioners only break out spellcraft when the situation seems to seriously call for it, while other witches regularly cast spells for all kinds of things. It has to be said that many witches feel that spellcraft is a defining characteristic of a witch and that it's questionable to call yourself one if there's no spellcraft in your practice at all. I'm only telling you what's what, though – don't shoot the messenger!

A witch usually sees themselves as working with the power obtained from *within*, tapping into that power in order to move through personal challenges or spread positivity outward. Although many witches also work with powers that they see as external, such as spirit guides, deities or energies from nature, they hardly ever attribute the results of their workings to those external forces *alone*. They often see the internal power as truly significant. This nod to personal empowerment helps us to recognize how potent we are, and this really helps with self-esteem and also encourages us to take accountability and get shit done!

Many witches follow agreed group guidelines or operate within traditions, and this can obviously be effective. Witches may choose to follow meticulously the instructions laid out for them in books, on websites, by online mentors or within their local communities. Again, these strategies can be extremely effective. I'd never say it's wrong to follow an existing framework. This book, however, is more about sewing a high-powered patchwork quilt of your own devising, featuring different facets of culture, art and all manner of personal interests and references. Drawing on your own energy, power, passion, will and capability, these elements will provide the fuel for the manifestation of your desires.

WHAT DOES "WITCH" REALLY MEAN?

Due to the emphasis on personal power, "witch" is a word that tends to pick up political and radical overtones during times of cultural upheaval. In the face of division, extremism and threat to the planet, the idea of being a witch gathers attention. Many witches currently see the label as a way of professing their willingness to take responsibility into their own hands, fighting for justice and ensuring they're not siding with any kind of system or institution that denigrates others or harms the planet. For some, "witch" is a label that indicates rebellion against inequality. It is seen as a word that naturally connects to the experience of oppression, offering a strengthening elixir to help in the battle against it. For others, it is preposterous to suggest that witchcraft has any place in a political discussion, as you can be a witch and be in the most privileged position in the world and hold any political views. Magick is, like electricity, seen as a neutral force that can be harnessed for all kinds of intentions – good, bad and very ugly! But it's not surprising that a connection has been made between witchcraft and the fight for change and social justice, because witches have always been on the fringes and viewed as outsiders. We often call on the burning core of our power and bravery in order to stand up to oppression. Witches who want to get shit done know that their connection to spirit, energy and magick can make all the difference in the very real battles being waged in the real world.

I have met many witches and they seem to share some threads in common. Many of them knew from a young age that they had some kind of leaning toward mystical activities and spiritual experiences. They often see their spiritual practice as a way to enhance life and cope with reality. They do not separate spirituality from the flesh and blood, "real world" stuff, but instead utilize it to make changes there. They tend to err on the side of personal accountability and a belief in their inherent power to do great things. Witches feel connected to what is beyond the cognitive. They recognize that they have experiences for which they cannot show workings or proof, and they choose to be comfortable with those experiences and document them to see if they can improve upon them, rather than pretending they never happened. Witches tend to believe that they are invested with the same power

LET'S BEGIN

and complexity as animals, plants and the entire terrain of Earth itself which, incidentally, they usually see as humanity's sacred home to which we owe love and respect.

Witches don't all conform to the same attitudes and principles. You will come across witches who are at the opposite end of the spectrum to you in many different ways, yet you both practise the craft. No one owns the word "witch", much to the frustration of those who would like to see themselves as its gatekeepers. When you take the word as a descriptor for yourself, it will be for your own set of reasons. As long as those reasons make sense to you, no one can take that decision out of your hands or tell you "no". But if you decide to take the word "witch" for yourself, you'll have a much better time if you know, in your own heart, that you do so from a place of authenticity.

WRITE IT

◊ What are the various reasons that someone might be fearful or uncertain about claiming the word "witch" for themselves?

◊ How are you feeling about the word "witch" at this point in your life and why?

◊ In your opinion, what does it mean to be an authentic witch?

TRY IT

◊ Check out some videos, podcasts or articles from witches sharing their personal journey of claiming and using the word "witch" for themselves. What do you notice about their experiences? What interests you most about their decision to call themselves witches?

◊ Make a timeline that records your awareness and understanding of the word "witch", from the first few times you heard it in childhood to now. Don't worry if some of your beliefs about witches were fearful or judgemental. The timeline will show you the journey you have taken to arrive here as a reader of this very witchy book!

WHY BE A REBEL WITCH?

Carving a path that winds around your psyche and goes to the door of your heart is a guarantee of potent results. The more you put *yourself* into the witchy system you create, the more the system will provide for you. The unique collection of influences and references to which you've been exposed throughout your life so far will empower and inspire you. This material can be mined to create a super-strong practice that could never be replicated by anyone else in all of space and time. Ain't that fancy?! Only YOU will know why you choose to listen to a certain song while preparing to do spellcraft, or why there's an image of a certain comic book character on your altar. Only YOU can say why a battered horror story book from your adolescence is your number one sacred text. As a rebel witch, you get to construct a practice that includes all the concepts and vibes that made you feel fizzy during your darkest times. You get to unlock and immerse yourself in a practice that captures the memories of your most dizzying highs and your most 'out there' visions of the future!

If your path has a shrewdly personalized design, it will contain the elements of power that speak most keenly to your soul, representing your beliefs, experiences and intentions. Casting spells and performing rituals from the epicentre of such a consciously carved practice will really make them count. The more you use the music, colours, objects and words that genuinely matter to you, the greater the chance that you'll call in the results you envision. After all, simply borrowing what others have created will find you trying to use ideas that reflect *their* power, not *yours*. If something doesn't feel relevant to you, and you're only adopting it because you feel you should or because it works for someone else, you're missing the chance to connect with your practice at heart level. Pack your workings with your personal symbolism and the results will speak for themselves.

Constructing a deeply personalized practice is also likely to ensure commitment and longevity. Other people's practices can temporarily tantalize, but in the long term they seem to gather dust and go dull precisely because they weren't generated from within. There's no point in following another witch's instructions for casting spells if you actually find their technique long-winded, too complicated or filled with language that you don't really vibe with. There's no point in setting up an altar space that looks like someone else's and doesn't take your tastes into consideration. Taking on another witch's beliefs about anything in the craft without asking yourself what you think is a sure way to find yourself hitting a dead end. Maybe later you'll tell yourself that you just "had a witchy phase" that didn't last because your heart wasn't in it. But in reality, you just hadn't given yourself the chance to be a witch on your terms, in a way that honours who you are.

Designing something that excites you means you'll go back to it weekly, monthly, yearly. It will continue to enthral you and it will stay relevant. The great thing about drawing your ideas from within is that they will look and feel like something you want to keep touching and dancing with. Witchy concepts and aesthetics can go through phases, as you may have noticed if you've searched for videos or images relating to witchcraft on social media. People do tend to be influenced by what they see in the realm they inhabit, whether consciously or unconsciously, and sometimes particular things "stick" and gather momentum. But something you see online or read about in a book could turn out to be a flash in the pan rather than a lasting source of inspiration. Being dedicated to creating your own path from the ground up means that you can allow yourself to be inspired if you come across an element that speaks to you, but only if it's really backed up by a deep personal accordance with it.

When it comes to self-discovery, creating your own thing on your own terms is key! As you progress on your rebel witch path, you will discover so many hidden and forgotten rooms in your psyche, and you can explore them freely, fascinated by what you find. You will deepen into the richness and strangeness of who you are. Through seeing what works for you in witchcraft, you can come to see what you need more of in your life overall, as well as what you have grown out of or come to dislike. As you change over time, your practice will shift to fit your new shape, and that will also be an illuminating experience. As you own your sovereign craft, you will dare yourself to try new things and embolden yourself to have a practice that is uber-authentic. This means pushing yourself out of any comfort zone you may have previously hung on to in your spiritual life. It means authenticity without apology. It means you don't have to wait for a permission slip from anyone else, and that could be a big levelling-up process for you.

If you find yourself at a point in life where things are a little more crunchy than they are smooth, your practice will become your happy place. As you can fill it with the stuff that really speaks to you, it can comfort you when you're feeling down. Perhaps following a uniquely personal spiritual path will also serve to remind you that you needn't quietly persevere with something that constantly leaves you feeling unsatisfied or miserable; this in turn may cause you to gather the confidence required to leave a soul-crushing situation or demand more for yourself in life. You never know where the journey of being a rebel witch might take you. It doesn't stop at the edge of your sacred space. The results will spill over into every part of your everyday life.

WRITE IT

◊ What kinds of benefits are you most excited about experiencing as you journey along your path as a rebel witch?

TRY IT

◊ Close your eyes, take some deep breaths and say aloud a few times, "I am carving a path that winds around my psyche and goes to the door of my heart." Try saying this (or other words of power with a similar meaning) whenever you need to centre yourself into your witchy sovereignty.

3

THE CHALLENGES OF BEING A REBEL WITCH

Becoming part of an already existing witchcraft tradition can provide a sense of ease and comfort. Following any set of instructions on witchcraft can have that effect, especially if those instructions have been around for a while and have earned respect. For many practitioners, it feels safer to adopt what has already been prescribed by a traditional framework or voice of authority, and for others it is just less labour-intensive and therefore feels like a more sensible route. When you decide to heavily personalize each aspect of your craft, you sacrifice the simplicity and clarity that comes from having a path already laid out and waiting for you. You may experience feelings of insecurity and doubt because you're out there alone, carving a structure to fit your specifications. No one is going to sign off on what you make, and no one can nod in agreement at how effective it is. There's no top-down knowledge stream to make you feel like you're in safe hands. While that might sound freeing, it can be weirdly oppressive in its own way!

It takes more time to work out how any aspect of the craft might be reimagined from your unique perspective, rather than just following the advice from a book, video or coven leader, so you have to get used to the time drain! It can take a while to construct your practice, so your patience might be tested at times while you decide which elements will be included or what order to do things in. Your path might get wonky, with setbacks, uncertainties and dead ends along the way, as you try to figure out what you want to build and why. You might feel vulnerable or weirded out at times, adjusting to the practice you are creating, and there will be no one to turn to who follows precisely the same path and can totally empathize or encourage you onward.

One thing that can be hard to navigate is the "magpie eye" that so many witches have. (It's very common!) When you allow yourself to adventure freely through all kinds of influences in your practice, you may find that everything tastes so good and you want to include it all. It can be thrilling that your practice contains quirky elements that distinguish it from others, but the downside is becoming fixated on adding new things or just being unwilling to put anything down if it excites you even remotely. A rebel witch with a magpie eye runs the risk of a cluttered practice in which the intentions have become muddy and there's a suffocating sense of overkill. Only you can decide if there are too many different activities, studies or focus areas in your practice. Some witches can handle multiple altar spaces, a handful of deities and quite a few magickal workings going on at once before they start to feel swamped. But that doesn't make their jam-packed journey superior to one that's a lot less busy. Witches with time constraints or high demands on their attention may not feel that they can regularly get to every spinning plate on a regular basis, so the obvious solution is to have fewer of them spinning in the first place.

Building something that reflects where you've been and what's important to you is bold. And boldness can be hard to sustain. You have to believe that what you create can be effectual and that you don't need to defer to someone else to tell you what's what. If you're a person who struggles with low confidence, self-esteem issues or

LET'S BEGIN

impostor syndrome, you may get pushback from yourself when trying to implement your own rules, telling yourself that your ideas don't hold weight and that others know best. You'll need to fight through this mentality and keep going. You'll need to state words of power as you hold your hand over your heart or look in the mirror, reminding yourself that there's so much majesty in being your own magickal monarch! You'll need to keep pushing yourself to put your theories into practice and follow your curiosity instead of convincing yourself simply to imitate what someone else is doing. Don't forget that you can actually cast spells to help you develop more confidence and perform rituals to strengthen self-belief. What about a spell that includes a visualization or written story in which you are a self-confident hero? Or a ritual that includes a song, dance or other artistic piece to symbolize confidence filling you and fear leaving you? Explore the chapters on spell and rituals in Part II (see pages 145–84) and find delicious creative ways of constructing spells for confidence and so much more.

If you choose to expose anything about your path, you need to be prepared for some questioning, pushback or ridicule from both within and outside the witchy community. There will always be someone with something to say. For many who choose to structure a wild and uncommon practice, it's a wondrous training in confident ownership of their ideas. But learning to believe in your inventions is hard, and others can say things that make you feel like you're going to falter. It can be hard enough to convince yourself that it's OK to have your favourite kid's toy on your altar or to make sexy lingerie into your preferred ritual dress. If you lose sleep worrying about how others would or could judge your decisions, you'll become stuck in an unsatisfying in-between place, never really taking the necessary leaps to grow as a witch. So it's about making that daily commitment to explore beyond *your* comfort zone and potentially *also* beyond the comfort zones of others!

When creating a uniquely designed path, some witches may struggle to take themselves seriously. If you're leaving an established religious faith and moving into being a rebel witch, you may have this nagging

THE CHALLENGES OF BEING A REBEL WITCH

feeling that your previous belief structure was somehow much more legitimate than any you could devise for yourself. You may find yourself mocking or questioning your self-created path because it's just something you "made up". But the truth is that you can inject it with so much meaning and potency, threading it through with all that excites you most in life. That's spiritual rocket fuel, poptart! Imagine how much your life will be enhanced by that. Each time you demean your path by telling yourself it doesn't count, remind yourself that it's composed of everything that makes you feel fizzy, fierce and ready to be the ruler of your own galaxy!

WRITE IT

◊ What setbacks or downsides might you encounter and how do you intend to deal with them?

◊ How do you know you're ready to be a rebel witch, creating your own path rather than following any pre-existing system?

◊ *"Discerning the difference between what is a passing surface interest and what holds deep significance for you is the key to knowing what to add to your practice."* Write about your emotional response to this statement.

TRY IT

◊ Imagine a strong, sacred wall of defence and protection around a vibrant rainbow structure that represents your rebel witch practice. The wall guards your practice at all times, symbolizing your willingness to believe in what you are building and to give your practice consistent nourishment even though others may not understand or agree with it. You can bring this image to mind whenever your practice feels threatened and needs protection.

◊ Start to consciously notice when you seek validation or ask for permission from others. As a rebel witch, you will be looking at the pre-existing traditions, practices and tendencies within the craft in order to see which rules you want to break and how you can make it your own. Dropping people-pleasing tendencies and permission-seeking behaviour across the board will help you to design what truly works for you in witchcraft and in life!

◊ For some tips on dealing with the challenges mentioned in this chapter and more, have a look at the troubleshooting chapter (see pages 236–44).

4

COMING OUT OF THE BROOM CLOSET

How important is it to be "out and proud" about your witchy practice? There's no right answer! Every witch must explore this question for themselves, and for some it's an essential part of the journey. Keeping such a significant spiritual path a secret feels weird and wonky for many witches. It can feel better to be transparent about spiritual beliefs. The whole process of publicly owning your witchy identity can be electrifying! Whether you're just telling a handful of key loved ones or starting social media platforms to invite the world into your practice, revealing that you're into the craft is a way of affirming your commitment to it. It often takes courage and confidence to step out of the broom closet, making it a meaningful rite of passage that demonstrates your sincerity. If you want to come out as a witch, you could start by speaking to one key person in your life about the ideas and practices you're exploring. See how that conversation goes and lean into what you think should happen next.

Then, you might feel like doing any of the following:

- Tell more people.
- Start expressing your witchy identity through your clothing and accessories.

- Have an altar space and/or some witchy imagery on display in your home.
- Leave witchy resources on your bookshelves.
- Post something about the craft on social media.
- Join a witchy discussion group on social media and/or follow witchy hashtags.
- Attend a relevant local event, such as a mind-body-spirit festival or a witchy gathering.
- Bring your spiritual beliefs/practices up in a conversation.

For others, stepping out of the broom closet could be highly disruptive and even unsafe. The stakes may be too high for witches from deeply religious households or conservative communities, so in order to protect themselves, they may have to keep their practice clandestine. They might emerge from the closet to only a handful of people, asking them to keep the information private so that it doesn't fall into the wrong hands. Let's face it, being able to open up to everyone in your life without any fear of reprisal is a massive stroke of good luck and not every witch finds themselves blessed in that way.

Having to keep a lid on your practice doesn't make you a less efficient or legitimate witch. In fact, incubating your practice and its processes in secrecy can be beneficial. Sometimes, telling too many people what you're doing risks encouraging their interference, or you might end up thinking overtime about how *others* perceive your path rather than focusing on what *you* need from it. Don't convince yourself that you *should* be out and proud about your witchiness. If you're the only one who knows about your path, then it's often easier to experiment and explore, knowing that you don't need to explain or justify anything. For some witches, stepping out of the broom closet would certainly incur a gigantic amount of judgement or a shit-ton of questions. So take all this into account before you decide how open you want to be. You might want to ask yourself the following questions:

- Who do I want to tell and why?
- How do I imagine/hope that leaving the broom closet will turn out?

COMING OUT OF THE BROOM CLOSET

- What would the worst outcome be and how would I react?
- What are the potential positive long-term effects of coming out as a witch?
- What are the potential negative long-term effects of coming out as a witch?
- Why is it important to recognize that I'm not obliged to leave the broom closet?
- How can I ensure that I still value my practice even if I don't leave the broom closet?

Don't pressure yourself to leave the safe confines of the broom closet too soon. If you're a brand-new witch, you're about to learn what it's like to be giddy about all the discoveries and experiences you're enjoying, and you might want to bubble over like a cauldron full of fizz! It's natural to want to share the stuff that's putting a spring in your step, but all that enthusiasm can also make for poor judgement. You don't want to end up wishing you'd kept quiet. If you fall in love with the witchy life, you'll likely live it for many moons to come, so there's no hurry to let people know straight away. Take your time and let yourself figure out the parameters of openness at a sensible pace.

Of course, we don't just leave the broom closet once – we leave it many times throughout our lives. You might be a seasoned practitioner, well known among family and friends for your magickal antics, and yet you'll still experience interactions that cause you to weigh up the pros and cons of openness. Maybe your instinct will tell you that you're not in witch-friendly territory and you'll refrain from mentioning it in the context of a conversation about spiritual beliefs. Perhaps you'll want to wait a while before telling a new friend or colleague. Maybe you'll keep a separate social media account for the more in-depth spiritual stuff so you feel you can really let loose without certain sets of prying eyes to worry about. Whatever you decide, it's all about honouring your individual needs so that your practice can flourish without finding yourself in a pickle. No one is *owed* access to your spiritual journey. It certainly doesn't have to be a matter of public record and you're within your rights to calculate risk before letting the black cat out of the bag!

LET'S BEGIN

WRITE IT

◊ Write an account of your journey in and out of the broom closet so far. If you've only just started out on your path, you could write about your current intentions, musings and worries relating to coming out as a witch. If you're a more seasoned practitioner, you could write about decisions you've made regarding openness and secrecy along the way and why you made those choices.

TRY IT

◊ Research which areas of the world are unsafe for witches to go public. Learn about modern-day oppression of witches and laws surrounding witchcraft.

◊ Research other witches' accounts of their emergence from the broom closet. What can you learn from their stories? What are the differences between their stories and your own?

QUESTIONING THE CONSENSUS

Within the craft, there are many points of agreement between practitioners. A general consensus has been reached regarding things such as the uses of various herbs and crystals, the ways to carve out sacred space and the purposes of the different tools. There are common techniques and ideas that have stood the test of time and are used by all kinds of witches. Lists of correspondences for everything from flowers, trees and animals to colours, numbers and the phases of the moon are readily available to help witches understand the consensus around their meanings and uses in the craft. These lists can be a helpful way for beginners to get a handle on the potential uses of things, or to jog the memory of seasoned witches about ingredients and symbols for spells and rituals. But they also lure witches into the trap of lazy acceptance.

A consensus is often reached because of many witches trying the same thing and getting fizzy results. But shared experience can only ever point you in a potentially reliable direction – it can never be the deciding factor in whether or not you agree with the consensus on something. You can only receive that answer from your own personal experiences. There's nothing wrong with using the lists of correspondences for some strong starting points to begin your witchy experimentations. But you can also decide that such lists mean little to you and that you're not really interested in using them at all. Or you might want to try a middle ground, paying attention to certain items on a list and disregarding others.

As a rebel witch, you'll want to give yourself room to make your own assessments. Most lists of witchy correspondences will tell you that rose quartz is a stone that represents love and relationships. But you might have a piece of rose quartz yourself and find that the energy it gives off for you has more to do with success and ambition. A list of correspondences will often tell you that the new moon is the lunar phase most associated with new beginnings, mystery and potential. But you may feel that the new moon vibes seem to have more to do with protection and safeguarding, making it a useful phase for you to do magick based on those needs. Your direct feelings and experiences will override lists and instructions made by others. You might not even bother with crystals or moon phases at all because those things simply don't inspire you.

Questioning the consensus isn't about pointless rebellion against accepted standards – it's about valuing your personal perspective and knowing how powerful that perspective is. If you agree with the consensus around a specific ingredient or activity, then by all means go with the flow. If you don't see an issue with the idea of lavender being associated with rest and peacefulness, for example, then perhaps you won't see a need to rock that particular boat. After all, lavender is widely known to encourage sleep and promote lowered blood pressure, so it makes sense. But let's say that you associate lavender with a particularly inspiring, empowered aunt of yours who used to grow lots of it in her garden when you were young. In that case, you may see lavender as a plant that could conjure up her qualities of boldness and confidence, or help you connect with her spirit to have conversations with her. This is not wrong. It's an interpretation based on a weighty personal experience. That stuff counts. Overriding your life story and the many ways in which it has informed your outlook on things would only serve to dilute your magick and suck the sparkle from your personal witchcraft journey.

QUESTIONING THE CONSENSUS

You can question anything you hear in a video or podcast, or read in any book, including this one! Although a particular rule or standard might make sense for tons of witches, it might not make sense to *you*, and you're the only person performing your magickal workings, so your opinion holds the most weight when it comes to creating a strong, vibrant practice that *works*. Along the way, you're likely to come across heavy-handed resources and individuals with insistent voices, adamant that their ideas are the one absolute truth and the last word in witchcraft. You'll have to be strong to keep dialoguing with yourself about your own take on things rather than getting locked into this idea that others can dictate how you're shaping your craft.

So how should you use witchy resources? Should you sling them out altogether? Absolutely not! Imbibing witchy information can be inspiring and useful. But it's most effectual when you allow yourself to put it through the lens of your own experiences and opinions. I don't know about you, but I've never enjoyed having to adhere to something strictly just because it was upheld by those who came before me. Whenever you're looking up a list of correspondences online, enjoying a book about the craft or taking on information from a video, podcast or social media post, notice when you're feeling inspired or intrigued. Your body will often tell you when this is happening. You might get goosebumps, your shoulders and chest might puff outward, your eyes might widen as you lean in to read more, or you might feel a fizziness as you envision putting the suggestions into action. If something speaks to you deeply and you feel that you want to experiment with it or include it in your craft, that's when you know you're on the right track!

WRITE IT

◊ Write a statement of your commitment to question whether or not suggestions and information provided by others is right for you. Within the statement, include a section about why it's so useful and important to question the consensus and filter information through your own lens.

TRY IT

◊ Consider how your body and mind respond to any witchy information or suggestions that you absorb from books, websites etc. Notice when you are feeling inspired. What happens to your body? What happens to your mind? Notice when you are feeling turned off, uninspired or alienated by information you absorb. Again, what happens to the body and mind? This exercise will help you to figure out what intuitively resonates with you, making it easier to use resources to inspire your own design rather than as rulebooks to be strictly followed.

◊ When considering a piece of advice from a witchcraft book, video or other resource, ask yourself these questions: "Could this be more helpful to me if it was tweaked in some way?"; "What do I like about the idea and what doesn't resonate?"; "How could I change the technique/perspective so that it's more authentic for me?"; "Could the technique/perspective actually help me with my personal aims?"

6

MAKING IT YOUR OWN

There is only one version of you in the whole of space and time. You are your own thing! Nothing before or after will ever be the exact same as you. Although you can empathize with many experiences and feelings that others have, only you have lived your exact life. Only you have access to what makes you a unique individual, and you will never be replicated. The personal knowledge that is only *yours* to use is among the most potent of your intellectual possessions. If your practice is cookie cutter, it's not going to work even half as well as if it's laden with pieces of yourself. The stuff you've personally taken to your heart will have far greater significance to you than anything someone else has recommended.

So, your rebel witch path will be invested with your essence. If you take anything from this book, let it be that! Bring in the things that mean the most to you: the colours, quotes, songs, clothes, genres, fictional characters, patterns, textures, foods, references and associations. Bring in the time of day that you love most, the seasons you enjoy, the animals, films, locations and concepts that resonate with you. Consider the historical events that have influenced you, the sounds and shapes and fears and fantasies that have defined you. Seriously – take an inventory of all the things that make you who you are, and that inspire you to become who you envision being!

Don't be afraid to figure out what makes you tick most of all and include it. In order to make your path as power-packed as it can be, you must permit yourself to put your unique stamp on it. This means mining your memory for the things you lived through which made you stronger, wiser, more joyful or more aware. It means embracing who you are, what you love and what really makes you shimmer! Try to do so without apology. Your path can include whatever makes your blood cells sing. You might see certain aesthetics and concepts being used by other witches and find that you don't vibe with them. Maybe you're not really a rustic, woodland type – maybe you're more about neon colours and modern imagery. You may want a simplified practice, uncluttered and straightforward, or you may be a maximalist witch who combines a hundred different things in kaleidoscopic harmony. Maybe you don't vibe with the idea of working with deities, celebrating moon phases or playing with Tarot cards, and you're not obliged to do any of those things just because they're popular. You decide what holds power for you, as you're the only one who will rely on your practice to make things happen in your life.

As you started your life, a timeline began to form. It's a timeline of everything that mattered to you in some way and made you who you are, good or bad. The timeline includes the events that shaped you, the goals you reached and the significant relationships that had an effect on your reality. It includes the times when you fell in love – with people or certain types of music or activities – and when you moved to new places. It records when you entered new phases of your life. Some of the stuff on the timeline continues to this day, while other stuff came to an end, despite still mattering greatly to you now. This is a timeline of the things that changed you, broke you, repaired you and illuminated you. It will be important on your witchcraft journey. Rather than risking the creation of a cookie-cutter practice that doesn't truly align with who you are, you can decide to design a path that includes your absolute favourite things and honours your best and worst times. Your practice will be the only one of its type. Although it may share certain aspects in common with other witches' paths, it will be genuinely yours by virtue of the inclusion of your timeline into its tapestry. If you take the time to figure out what really empowers and inspires you, you can make space for it in

MAKING IT YOUR OWN

your path. If you are willing to embellish your path with deeply personal details, you will achieve the most meaningful results.

Remember that your personality type counts for so much when you're designing an effective path for yourself. Tweak everything so that it makes sense for who you are as an individual. Could you be described as extroverted and highly communicative? Or more introverted and reserved? Are you adventurous? Highly organized? Ambitious? Passionate? Impatient? Fussy? Inventive? Sophisticated? Lazy? Hilarious? Radical? Serious? Generous? There is no *wrong* personality type for witchcraft. What usually causes a problem is when witches attempt to shoehorn themselves into a practice that doesn't reflect and complement who they are. If you prefer things sweet and simple, let your decisions as a witch reflect that. If you like things loud and larger than life, shape your path accordingly! There are minimalist witches and maximalist witches, as well as those who fall in the middle somewhere; don't be afraid to figure out where you are on that spectrum. If you like to work to a fairly unshakeable schedule and have things planned out way in advance, honour those characteristics within your craft. More of a chaotic, spontaneous type who just likes to see where the days take you? Your practice can reflect that.

Maybe you feel wary of jumping into the creation of a highly individualized practice, filled with the random wonders inside your mind and all the things that make you who you are. You may tell yourself that whatever is pre-existing, tried 'n' tested, and widely recognized is always going to hold more power, and that you ought to just learn it, follow it and avoid going too far off the beaten track. But if you're reading this book, you're probably willing to shift your perspective. You're aware of the great power inside your very own story – the power that has always been available to you. You know that this power is inherent in you and that it doesn't need to be tied to any external traditions in order to be valid. Of course, there's nothing wrong with following traditional customs and procedures in spirituality, and there are resources to help you learn them. But this book is intended to help you construct something of yourself – a witchcraft practice that looks and feels like you.

LET'S BEGIN

WRITE IT

◊ Figure out the timeline of the significant events and influences in your life. Include meaningful conversations, game-changing events and powerful relationships. Include the positive, the negative and everything in-between. Include the discovery of important music, films or books as well as undeniably potent one-off experiences that changed the shape of your soul. Include times that you fell in love with certain ideas or changed your personal style, joined a band, left a job, got your heart broken – all the stuff that made any kind of impact! You might want to type this on an electronic device rather than writing it on paper, so you can keep updating the document, adding more things as you remember them.

TRY IT

◊ Start asking people in your life what has inspired, influenced or changed them over the course of time. Notice what they say when faced with this question. See if this inspires you to decide which influential things you want to include in your craft.

◊ Consider any literature, visual art, film etc that heavily references the creator's personal experiences. How does this work make you feel? How do you think it may have helped those creators to work through such personal details in their work? You could see the creation of your own witchy path as a similar form of creative endeavour into which you pour your personal experiences and beliefs.

◊ Start noticing your personality traits and considering how your witchy path can be constructed to complement them rather than working against them. As people change over the course of time, consider if your idea of your own personality might be stuck in the past. Pay attention to your current personality traits rather than assigning old, outdated labels to yourself.

◊ As you go through the rest of this book, keep your individual quirks and needs in mind. Remember that you can customize any suggestion to make it more applicable to you. If an idea will sparkle more if you put your personalized stamp on it, then don't hold back.

WHY WITCHCRAFT?

What are you hoping for, results-wise, from being a witch? What do you visualize for yourself? How can you see your life potentially improving? New witches can consider these questions, but it's also worth asking yourself even if you've been practising for decades! Your aims and desires change as you do, calling you to reassess your direction as you go along. Doing anything just for the sake of it doesn't allow you to get excited about your progress. How can you know if witchcraft is working for you unless you've established what you're hoping to get out of it?

Here are some of the key reasons that people become witches:

To feel stronger and more empowered

Using spells, rituals and other witchcraft components in order to cope with life's challenges gives you a whole extra toolkit for life, reminding you that you're capable of dealing with your problems and powering up when you need to.

To connect with nature and natural forces

Do you feel that the world around you is filled with potency, vibrancy, energy? Do you want to feel more connected to the land you live on, the sky above you, the animals, the roots of plants and trees plunging down into the soil, the planets orbiting the sun? You can draw from the power of these things in your practice, as many witches do.

To build self-esteem

As you see yourself increasing your witchy power, making things happen and relishing each step on the journey, your self-esteem will grow. It's hard to keep feeling bad about yourself when your witchcraft is blossoming and you're getting stronger and stronger in your practice.

To promote self-discovery

The things you can learn about yourself as a witch are endless. I've discovered so much about my interests and tastes, my spiritual skills, my emotions, my fears and insecurities and how to deal with them. My spiritual path has given me insights into how my past has affected me and what to release from my life or welcome into it. Witchcraft has been a part of my healing journey. If you want to delve deeply into your inner workings, being a witch can give you many opportunities to do so.

To heal wounds and feel happier

Witchcraft can be a truly healing force. It gives you lots of creative ways to receive the things you want, get rid of what's not working and figure out what to do when you're lost. It is a path with massive potential to increase your happiness.

To take revenge and right wrongs

It can be hard to feel empowered when cruelty and injustice occur. Witchcraft gives you an avenue to help justice materialize in situations where you would otherwise feel dwarfed by the might of the wrongdoer. Casting spells and performing rituals can be a part of your action plan for fighting injustice and putting things right.

LET'S BEGIN

To bring in money, success, love, health, etc

Spells are a tool to get what you want. Decide what you desire and design spells to bring that stuff in. One of the most beautiful aspects of witchcraft is that it gives you a creative, exciting way to make your life better.

To satisfy curiosity – see what's really possible!

If you have a keen desire to find out if you can really cast spells, connect with gods or read Tarot cards, there's only one way to find out! You don't lose anything by giving it a go.

To become a better human being

As a witch, you have the opportunity to do workings to help others. You can also help *yourself* to grow, learn and change. You get to use your powers to do good things for people and for the planet if you want to.

To help and heal others

Cast spells to help your loved ones get what they want. Use your Tarot cards or crystal ball to help people figure out what their next steps should be. Work with the energy in a tense situation to help everyone involved feel calmer and more willing to empathize with each other. The possibilities for being of service to others as a witch are boundless.

To protect and shield property and loved ones

Being a witch means you have extra options for protecting your belongings and loved ones, on top of the precautions that everyone takes. Spells can form strong energetic barriers around the things and people you love.

To fuel activism and social justice

You can use witchcraft to help you power up for your chosen activism. When you commit to making a difference in the world, it helps to have a spiritual practice that inspires you, encourages you to keep going and fuels you for the fight ahead.

To connect with other witches to do collaborative work

You can get involved with witchcraft communities in your area and/ or online to discuss how to improve your practice, exchange ideas or form a coven to combine your magickal efforts. There's always an interesting discourse around witchcraft, so you can get involved with the discussions and have your say on the hot topics of the moment.

To complete creative projects

For those with a tendency to start strong and then fizzle out before the finish line, witchcraft can help. A ritual to express your commitment can inspire you to keep going. You can receive guidance from non-physical beings to help you figure out how to overcome issues. You can even cast a spell to protect a project and make it a roaring success.

To find answers to life's deep questions

Exploring a spiritual practice and the philosophy behind it can give you a sense of deepening understanding. It's easy to feel lost, small, confused and overwhelmed. While I'm not claiming that such feelings aren't understandable or that they can be completely eradicated, I will say that after so many years of practising witchcraft, I know how much it helps me when I'm feeling those kinds of emotions.

To increase self-expression and authenticity

"Witch" feels like an undeniably authentic label for me. It expresses a lot about who I am, what brings me joy and how I want to conduct myself. For many witches, practice of the craft feels like such a potent piece of their self-expression that nothing else could replace it.

LET'S BEGIN

To make life more interesting

Look, I'm just going to be honest – aside from anything else on this list, being a witch is fun. Witchcraft can be highly creative, and it puts a compelling twist on even the most mundane of tasks. I get such a kick out of just sitting at my altar and lighting some candles. I love talking about the craft, reading about the craft, and don't even get me started on designing rituals and casting spells!

Establish how many of the items on this list apply to you, and consider things I haven't thought of. Knowing what you want from your adventure helps you recognize when to celebrate wins. It's thrilling to see that your individually designed witchy path is actually working for you and having clear aims will help you to confirm that. Be prepared to check in with your adventure as you go along to figure out if you're getting the results you originally desired. Over time, your reasons for being a witch can change, so revisit this question when necessary. It doesn't hurt to remind yourself regularly of why you want to be on this path.

If you find yourself leaning into this exploration of your reasons, you may want to consider creating a full document that outlines your motivations, intentions and commitments in your craft – both short-term and long-term. This document can be referenced during times of confusion and inaction, becoming a potent tool for keeping you on track. You can refer to it when you need direction, reading it aloud in front of a mirror for extra fizziness if you fancy! Here are the beginnings of some power-inducing statements that you can choose to add into your witchy document. Tweak where necessary.

- To me, being a witch means ...
- My strongest intention as a witch is ...
- The feelings that witchcraft will bring into my life are ...
- The feelings that witchcraft will decrease in my life are ...
- Issues that may arise are ...
- The tools I will use to avoid/decrease issues are ...
- Witchcraft will help me to achieve ...

WHY WITCHCRAFT?

- As a witch, I am fully committed to ...
- As a witch, I will always ...
- As a witch, I will never ...
- As a witch, I will pursue ...
- As a witch, I will avoid ...
- I expect my witchcraft journey to ...
- Some of the main things I want to learn on my journey are ...
- My short-term goals are ...
- My long-term goals are ...
- Some strong reasons to continue on my journey include ...

Don't worry if you can't finish some of these sentences yet. In Part II, we're going to get into the possibilities for the construction of your practice, and you may gain some clarity about your aims once you've become more aware of what these possibilities are.

WRITE IT

◊ Make your list of the things you want to achieve as a witch, changes you want to see in your life etc. You might want this list to be part of a longer document, outlining your motivations and aims as well as the things you may wish to avoid along the way, your chosen witchy rules and so on. The document can be simply a few powerful key statements, such as some of the examples given above, to offer direction along the way, or it can be a super-thick record of every single witchy intention and aim, going into fine detail! If you create this as an electronic document, you can make changes as you go along.

LET'S BEGIN

TRY IT

◊   Close your eyes, take a few deep breaths and take some
    time to visualize how your life will look a year from now,
    two years from now, in five years and in ten years, all as
    the result of practising your craft. Use your imagination
    to see beautiful images of success, peace, progress and
    happiness in whatever form feels right for you.

Statement of Power: The actions I take as a witch are empowered and filled with unique meaning. I do not take orders or subscribe to trends. I do what adds value and leave the rest, knowing that I am the best judge of the actions that will have the highest impact at any time.

Part II

MAKE IT HAPPEN

In Part II, we're getting into the nuts and bolts of the witchcraft practice. We'll look at the different things you can consider including in your own path, taking a tour of everything from spellcraft and ritual to magickal books and divine beings. Along the way, I'll offer you lots of pointers on how to experiment, get creative and incorporate all the twists, turns and secret colours of your once-and-only perspective into your own practice.

8

YOUR WITCHY CALENDAR

If the thought of scheduling too far ahead makes you feel bored or nauseous, that's OK. Maybe you're the kind of witch who likes to be surprised by your next move without anything feeling fixed or rigid. You could let *every* day be a totally free space with nothing on your witchy agenda. Some witches wake up and just *know* that they want to do a deity devotional, a house cleansing or a ritual for the rainforest. An idea springs out of them and they go with it. They prefer to let their actions and results unfold naturally, without having them pencilled into a calendar. Other witches love to get specific about their intentions for months into the future, especially if they closely follow the eight Sabbats that we're about to examine, or if they're big into astro struff.

Personally, if I didn't do *any* forward planning for my craft, I wouldn't be writing this book because I wouldn't be a witch at all. I am simply way too down the rabbit hole for an average day to be productive without some kind of to-do list. Linear time is a struggle for me. I'm often daydreaming and star gazing, with "one foot in the street and the other in the Milky Way", as Patti Smith once put it. My sticky relationship with the clock makes planning necessary in my craft and in every other aspect of my life. Another reason I tend to plan what I'll be doing on my witchcraft journey is because I love to have stuff to look forward to. There are key points of powerful observation on my yearly calendar with lots of room for random shenanigans in between. I personally observe about half of the eight Sabbats each year, plus usually observing the full moon each month, and I like to consider in advance what I'd like to do for those times and make some notes to help me visualize it. I also plan for some of the Marian feast days (because I work with the Holy Mother Mary). I observe a sprinkling of the birthdays of my favourite artists and rock stars, and some days of remembrance and awareness etcetera. Most of my spells, rituals and in-depth card readings are also put into my calendar because they are pre-planned.

But you can find your own way of doing it, dollface. Your craft, your rules – or lack thereof. I'm just going to outline a few things you may want to consider if you're the type to plan and schedule workings and other activities. You may not resonate with the notion of having fixed occasions within your yearly witchcraft practice at all, and that's OK! The rebel witch process is about giving yourself permission to take seemingly sacred, non-negotiable things off the table completely if the fancy takes you! But before you throw the concept of a calendar out entirely, consider how exciting it can be to have certain times during the year to look forward to – birthdays are a good example. Returning to an occasion year after year can deepen the meaning of life itself.

The Wheel of the Year

You get different vibes as the seasons change, right? For most, the season of spring has this hopeful, optimistic vibe and a sense that life is coming into being everywhere and hurtling into the future. Green shoots and delicate flowers come up and animals tentatively wake from hibernation. Summer tends to be based on celebration, extroversion, joy and connection with others outside in the heat, as we feel that an energetic pinnacle has been reached. Autumn offers a feeling of going inward, appreciating the internal voice more as the nights grow shorter and we stay indoors. The leaves change and fall, the colours shift, and your mood follows suit, turning to reflection and nostalgia. Winter can make us less energetic, as hormonal changes from lack of sunlight make us crave sleep. This time of year can be about retreating and focusing on projects in your home and in your mind, as well as taking much-needed rest. It can be a haunting and bleak season that encourages us to create warm, cosy situations with hot chocolate and blankets.

Of course all of these descriptions are from the perspective of someone who lives in a temperate region with four distinct seasons in a year. You'll have to consider the kinds of collective vibes around the seasons you experience, depending on where you are in the world! Plus, our individual emotional responses to the seasons are so personalized. I used to despise the summer for being so hot and sweaty and full of social events, whereas now I actually love all of the seasons for their particular qualities. Perhaps you've had similar shifts in the way you view the seasons too. As you evolve and weave memories into the tapestry of your life, the changing seasons of the year can slightly shift their meanings as they come around again and again.

The annual cycle of celebrations known as the Wheel of the Year is used by tons of witches to help them navigate their way through the seasonal energies around them. The Wheel can be a tool for keeping track of how your year is going, what you're grateful for and what's next for you. Many witches also feel that the Wheel connects them with the land they live on, encouraging them to notice the cycles of nature and marvel at the wonders of Planet Earth. The Wheel consists of eight festivals, known as Sabbats, symmetrically studding the year with jewels of reverence and celebration. For each occasion, you can check in with goals, perform relevant rituals and spells, and honour the land and any deities you may work with, etc. A bunch of witches who have very different beliefs and styles of practice may still be able to agree that the Wheel is a smashing spiritual device. Although not all witches follow the Wheel by any means, plenty do. You may find that some Sabbats do catch your eye and others fall a little flat, so you might want to try recognizing only the ones that feel fizzy. Perhaps none of the Sabbats will tickle your pickle and you'll start from scratch with annual observances of your own making. You have a delicious amount of creative freedom here, honey bee!

MAKE IT HAPPEN

At the times that these different observances were dreamed up, agriculture, keeping livestock and hunting your own food were still central to most people's daily lives. It's fair to say that this made the changes in the weather conditions way more significant than they are today. People were aware of their reliance on the seasons for a plentiful harvest, they had to keep food stored to make it through the harsh winters, and the occasions they focused on had a direct relationship to their livelihoods and survival. You could argue that it's important for witches to use the Wheel of the Year to ensure that they remain as connected to Earth's cycles as they can. But we can also be real and acknowledge that it just isn't common for things like crop growth, harvest time, animal hibernation and mating season to come up in everyday chats these days.

As a rebel witch, you can view the Wheel of the Year as a tasty blueprint for your own design, if you like. Placing a modern lens over the Wheel can have powerful results. If you choose to reimagine each Sabbat into something that honestly reflects your own concerns and experiences, then you'll be left with eight yearly opportunities to affirm your practice and your existence in a way that makes total sense to you.

Four of the Sabbats have Anglo-Saxon origins – the solstices and equinoxes. Solstices mark the shortest and longest day in each year, while equinoxes mark the points in each year when day and night are equal. The other four Sabbats are of Celtic origin and they mark significant seasonal changes, occurring at the midpoint between each Solstice and Equinox. The equinoxes and solstices technically occur at precise moments during the Sun's cycle, so the day can vary slightly from year to year. But it's fair to say that all eight Sabbats can be celebrated over at least two days, as you may do some observances the night before the official Sabbat date, on the day itself and afterwards if you wish. If you're anything like me, you probably want just about any kind of celebration to be extended for as long as possible.

YOUR WITCHY CALENDAR

Imbolc/Candlemas

A celebration of the coming of the light out of darkness and impending spring
1–2 February

- We're often full of good intentions for New Year's resolutions, but January can be a dark, sleepy month that feels slow-going and doesn't seem to encourage living up to resolutions. Maybe Imbolc at the beginning of February could be seen as the time when the action really begins for each 12-month period. Could January be a period of preparation and adjustment, leaving Imbolc to be the symbol of the starting line of the calendar year? You could use Imbolc as a time for calling forth new ideas or realizations using spells or calling on beings for help.
- The emerging light could be symbolic of new understanding. Do you need to learn the basics of something new or research a familiar topic more deeply to become more proficient? Imbolc could be about welcoming the light of knowledge.
- You might like to think of Imbolc as a time when you can bring light and warmth to others by offering your time, skills or money to those in need.
- Imbolc's theme of emerging light could symbolize the strength or potential inside you – or someone else – and the use of magick and ritual to help that grow stronger.

Spring (Vernal) Equinox/Ostara/Easter

A celebration of the arrival of spring and the lengthening days
19–23 March

- As Ostara falls around the time when life is sprouting from the Earth and becoming apparent again, it could be a good opportunity to think about how you'd like to "come out". How could you be more bold, assertive or open? Is there a message you want to get out there to people, or a way to be more authentic?

- Ostara imagery often includes new-born animals such as lambs, ducklings and rabbits! How about choosing to see it as a time to focus on animal rights and ending animal cruelty? Or connecting to animal energy and finding animal spirit guides?
- The balance of light and dark could represent a balance of different aspects of your personality. How can you celebrate your own contradictions or complexities?
- That balance of light and dark can also symbolize the ways in which people view the same situation from different perspectives, which can cause conflict and misunderstanding. At Ostara, try to see things from other people's point of view.
- You could decide to associate Ostara with Easter themes. If you don't want to focus on the Christian story, why not just make the Easter bunny your Ostara deity? Who doesn't love that guy?! (I would be tempted to turn my Easter bunny into Frank from *Donnie Darko* - but maybe that's just me.)

Beltane/May's Eve & May Day

A fiery celebration of summer's energies
30 April–1 May

- Beltane invites you to connect with the element of fire, which can often symbolize passion and determination. Maybe Beltane could be the time for you to get excited about your passions again, or go out there and find new ones! This high-energy Sabbat welcomes you to consider what gets you all fired up. Which causes do you want to focus on in the world? Where do you need to take action in your life? Where have you had enough, and how will you instigate change?
- Choose a creative project to work on throughout the Beltane period. You could craft a poem, painting, interpretive dance

or inspiring speech – whatever takes your fancy. Soak up the
Beltane energies to make the project pop!

- Raise a glass and make a toast to whatever you most want to
celebrate in your life. (You can bless the beverage before sipping,
and it doesn't have to be alcoholic.)
- Fire can destroy. It's a scary element in that way! What do you
want to get rid of in your life? You could do a fiery celebratory
dance while imagining stomping the yucky stuff into the ground,
or visualize fire engulfing and consuming your problems.

Summer Solstice/Litha/Midsummer

*A celebration of the longest day, after which the darkness begins to increase
once more*
20–22 June

- As this is a symbolic turning point in the year, consider creating a
vision board or collage to represent your emotional and spiritual
response to the longest day and the giving way of light to darkness.
The collage/board could be on paper or cardboard, or you could use
Pinterest or collect images in a folder on your phone.
- This time of peak natural light can symbolize truth and
realization. I'd say this is a tiptop opportunity for doing a reading
that addresses your burning questions (see page 189 for more on
card reading).
- Midsummer is an opportunity for a night of gratitude, creativity,
spellcraft and ritual, complete with your favourite food and
drink, when you stay awake to greet the longest day.
- Make a toast to summer, thanking the season for its gifts to
you and your loved ones. Then perform a ritual to welcome the
returning darkness and cold, also honouring its qualities and
readying yourself for its arrival – even if you don't really feel
enthusiastic about it.

MAKE IT HAPPEN

- You could throw a big summer party in the realm of the imagination – so no holds barred. What kinds of decorations and food and drink will you have? Will there be a pool? Who is the DJ? Who are the guests of honour?

———

Lughnasadh/Lammas

A celebration of the beginning of harvest time
1–2 August

- Lughnasadh could be a good Sabbat for considering your actions and their consequences. "You reap what you sow", as they say, so connect with the harvest vibe and ask yourself, "What have my choices brought into being?" Perform ritual to help you accept or. understand past actions.
- How could you thank someone to whom you are grateful? Has anyone been particularly generous toward you or guided you in some way? Send them a thoughtful message and/or loving intentions.
- You could make a poppet of woven wheat sheaves, or one that's stuffed with wheat alongside other materials. The poppet could symbolize your willingness to receive goodness and nurturing. (See pages 119–20 for more information about poppets.)
- This Sabbat could be a good time to focus on the collective. What does your family (or chosen family) need right now? What about the concerns of other communities you're a part of, such as fandoms, support groups, online groups or sports teams? What do you need to harvest together? How can your magick and ritual invite it in?
- What kind of spiritual preparation could you do at this time to see you through the rest of the year? Maybe you'd like to do a protection spell over your projects or home for the months ahead. Or perhaps you could declutter and reorganize your witchy space, rearrange the altar for the season, and so on.

Where does focus need to be shifted back to your key priorities? How can you invite a strong finish to the year by putting magickal measures in place now?

Autumn Equinox/Mabon/Harvest Festival

The second harvest celebration and preparation for colder months
21–24 September

- Mabon, as the year tips into the colder, darker months, is an opportunity to treat yourself. Munch things that taste good. Wrap yourself in a nice warm blanket. Binge watch a series that you find comforting – the kind you go back to every now and again when you want to indulge. Go to the things that make you feel safe and comforted, as if you're getting into hibernation mode.
- Put magickal intention into the food you make, the chores you do and the seemingly mundane things that would usually be overlooked. Heighten the witchiness at this time. Really let deep intention permeate through everything.
- Throw a Mabon dinner party in the realm of the imagination. Is it a formal black-tie event for your favourite deities? Or what about a buffet for your most esteemed fictional characters? A corporate power brunch for your spirit guides, to discuss how they intend to help you smash your goals and feel amazing? See what you can cook up.
- Check in on others and on yourself as the season changes. The days are getting darker. For some – and maybe this includes you – the seasonal shift can bring a downturn in mood and wellness. Brainstorm with your people to decide what you can do to lift your spirits. If you need some help, Mabon is a good time to make sure you reach out for it. Make a list of the things that bring warmth and brightness to your autumn days – and keep adding to it.

- Make a Mabon food parcel and put some gorgeous witchy high vibes on it before delivering it to your nearest food outreach programme.

_____

Samhain/Halloween/All Hallows' Eve & All Hallows' Day

A celebration of witches' New Year and the thinning of the veil between living and dead
31 October – 1 November

- A key theme of Samhain is fear. Create a protection servitor to help you confront and examine your fears in safety (see page 80 for more on servitors).
- Perform a memorial ritual for any loved ones who have passed on. Play their favourite music, write a poem to read aloud to them or take a look at photos of them in their happy moments during life.
- What do you want to get rid of? Is there a bad habit, unhelpful mindset or deep fear that needs to go? You could use a candle to symbolize the thing you want to say *adios* to, burning it down while you visualize your life without its influence. Or maybe you could write on a piece of paper about the thing you want to do away with and then burn the paper in your cauldron.
- Going to a Halloween event? Put some witchy enchantment into your costume to make sure you have a great time and attract lush conversations with new people (or with that special spooky someone you've got a scarily big crush on).
- Samhain is seen as the spiritual New Year for witches. You could take some time to reflect on the 12 magickal months behind you, as well as your witchy plans for the next 12 months. What are you going to change about your practice? What are your key goals going to be?

_____

Winter Solstice/Yule/Midwinter

A celebration of the shortest day, after which the light begins to increase once more
21–23 December

- You could celebrate this time of year by writing a poem or speech for the darkness and the cold – for winter itself. Tell winter what it means to you and thank it for what it offers you.
- Perform a welcome ritual for the sunlight that is now going to increase again. Tell it how pleased you are to know that it's slowly returning and perhaps confirm some plans for the warmer months ahead, sending witchy intentions to those plans to strengthen and protect them.
- Play your favourite music, put on some warm clothes and hit those fairy lights. Make any altar spaces cosy and festive. Create a delicious wintry atmosphere. You could even give yourself a present for this festive time of year. (Make mine a Tarot deck from my lengthy wish-list, please!)
- What needs to be thawed out and brought back to life? Is there a talent or passion that you dropped ages ago but now want to connect with again? What about a friendship that's gone a bit quiet and needs some attention? A goal you want to refocus on? Try a ritual or spell to get things moving where they may have been frozen.
- Be a nerdy witch. Study the traditions that are associated with this time of year throughout the world and brush up on deities and other non-human beings connected to different festivals and traditions. And what were the Yuletide activities of the past?

———

So, that's my take on the basics of each Sabbat, honey bee! Maybe you've only just learned about the Wheel while reading this book or maybe you've been a witch for decades and you just skipped over the information because you've read countless descriptions of it in your time. Either way, you now have an opportunity to lean into what these eight occasions may mean to you at this point on your witchy journey.

WRITE IT

◊ In your view, how useful is it for you to have some recurring celebrations/markers for your witchy year? Try to explore your answer fully.

◊ How applicable could the Wheel of the Year be to your practice at the moment and why?

◊ What are the potential benefits of avoiding an annual calendar and instead just doing things day-by-day?

◊ Which of the Wheel of the Year Sabbats attracts you the most and why?

◊ Which of the Wheel of the Year Sabbats is least appealing to you and why?

TRY IT

◊ Make a plan for your celebration of the next Sabbat on the calendar at the time of reading this. Within the plan, include some traditional elements if you like, as well as some elements of your own invention that reflect your own feelings about the relevance and vibe of the Sabbat. Record your experience and your realizations.

◊ Gather more information about the eight Sabbats, researching online and/or in books. What do you notice about the way the Sabbats are described and how you feel when studying them? ◊

The Moon Phases and Esbats

The lunar cycle can help you to track your moods and recognize patterns in your life. It also helps with planning spell workings, rituals, dates and events, and even chores and errands. It's also one of the most stunning things you'll ever see in your natural life and it never gets old, am I right? I could just stare at the moon forever.

This high-powered orb is beloved by mystics and magick-makers the world over, so if you're a "moon person", you're in good company. For a rebel witch, it's all about deciding for yourself what kind of role the moon could play in your practice, if it's going to feature at all. The moon is believed to have a powerful effect on emotions, perception and spiritual insight, and the light of the moon offers cleansing and charging properties. Having said that, there are lots of other ways to bring those qualities into your practice, of course, and there's no pressure to put a lunar spin on things.

An Esbat is most commonly carried out when the moon is full. Esbats involve honouring the moon's power through poetry and dance, summoning lunar energy for use in spellcraft and also using the moon's light to cleanse witchy tools and other possessions, as well as the body and soul of a witch themselves. Powerful stuff!

The stages of the moon within the lunar cycle are:

MAKE IT HAPPEN

New/dark moon

This is when the moon is not visible. This phase can be associated with mystery, secrecy, protection and the preparation stage before any action or inspiration can come forth. It can be seen as an opportunity to plant the seeds of future plans or set strong intentions for what needs to be achieved before the next new moon comes. It can also be good for spellwork and rituals relating to protection, banishing and exposing or keeping secrets.

Waxing crescent

This is when the moon is moving toward being half-illuminated on its way to full brightness. It can be a good time for getting clearer about ideas, coming to a better understanding of situations and sharpening your planning and focus. This phase can help you prime yourself for serious action.

First quarter/half moon

Now the moon is half-illuminated on its way to full brightness. The increasing full moon (as opposed to the decreasing one) can be a good time to focus on overcoming challenges and witnessing your power in order to face difficulties. It can also be seen as the ideal lunar phase for restoring balance in life, promoting equality and seeking mutual agreement/understanding. It can also represent different parts of you working in tandem or being accepted fully.

Waxing gibbous

The moon is now over half-full but not quite at its full luminosity yet. Associated with development and increasing vision and ability, this phase is seen as helpful for manifesting what you desire or strengthening what's already there. If you're trying to help something grow, this phase is a strong contender for the time to make it happen.

Full moon

This is the big one! The full moon is considered a potent phase for seeing the full truth of something, or for accessing your complete power. It's also associated with gratitude for what has been manifested and is therefore an obvious time to give yourself credit for your efforts and recognize how far you've come. There can be an air of heightened awareness and bigger witchy vibes during this phase.

Waning gibbous

The moon now begins to move away from fullness and back toward its half-lit state again. This phase could be seen as a time to identify obstacles and decrease or remove them. Shed what's not useful, streamline your workflow and avoid focus on the negative stuff that's holding you back in life. Decluttering and organizing could be teamed with ensuring that your home, family, business etc are magickally shielded.

Third quarter/half moon

This is the half moon on the decrease, in contrast to the earlier increasing one, so the vibe can be seen as different, for sure. Balance, equality and duality can still be important themes, but you may also look at the switch back toward darkness as a good time for recognizing the shadows in situations or within yourself. You may find that owning your mistakes is easier at this time, and that means that releasing and moving beyond them may also be possible.

Waning gibbous

Moving toward the end of the cycle and into the next new moon, these final slices of nightly lunar shine are usually useful for goodbyes, endings and making space for something new to be built or taken to the next phase. This is also a time associated with big-picture thinking – looking back on the entirety of a situation to see what you learned and how to move forward. Tying up loose ends and accepting death are therefore juicy themes to be considered.

WRITE IT

◊ What does the moon mean to you?

◊ How do you think your personal perspective on the moon originated?

◊ Which moon phase appeals to you most of all and why?

◊ Which moon phase doesn't appeal strongly and why?

TRY IT

◊ There are many traditions, superstitions and folktales linked to the moon. Try researching some and see what kinds of insights your findings can offer.

◊ Imagine the moon is a conscious individual who can talk with you, and that the different moon phases represent the moon's various characteristics and moods. What would a conversation be like with the moon in each one of its phases? Which moon phase is the most outgoing? The funniest? The most moody?

◊ Discover your moon sign using an online birth-chart calculator (there are plenty available for free). Then, research what your moon sign means for you.

◊ Did you know that the moon spends two to three days in your zodiac sign? For many witches, it's important to know when the moon is passing through their sign because things tend to intensify, more power becomes available and they want to be extra-prepared to deal with issues as they arise. Try downloading a moon-phase app that shows you which sign the moon is in.

◊ The sun spends a number of weeks in each zodiac sign on rotation and other astrological movements are going on all the time, potentially affecting the course of our thoughts, decisions and life events. You may wish to start researching this in more depth if you have the deep instinct that astro information will be important for you when planning your witchy and mundane activities.

Your Birthday, Memorial Days and Other Personal Anniversaries

You might like to recognize your own birthday in some way as part of your yearly witchy observations. It's a great day to consider how you've evolved over the course of a complete year, both as a witch and in general. You could give yourself a reading (see page 189) and you could also gift yourself something, perform a self-honouring ritual or do a spell to welcome delicious, high-vibe stuff to the year ahead. Putting blessings into birthday nibbles and drinks could be a good idea too (see page 167 for more on blessings and how to use them). There are so many rituals associated with birthdays, but they're all fed to us by family and society, and they don't always resonate with us as individuals. Choosing personalized rituals to honour your birth could help the day become a point of power on your calendar.

Within the timeline of your life, there could be other dates of major importance to you to factor into your annual witchy calendar. On the birthdays of key loved ones, such as children and partners, you may want to do rituals or spells for them, give thanks for the joy that they bring to you, and so on. Or you could do something witchy to mark a marriage or other relationship anniversary – and invite your partner/s to join in if they're open to your woo-woo ways!

There might also be certain days when you commemorate the lives of deceased loved ones. You may want to connect with them and ask them questions or feel their energy surrounding you – it depends on your beliefs about those kinds of possibilities. Whether you will be attempting a "cosmic phone call" to a deceased person or not, you can still decorate your altar in their honour using their favourite colours, some possessions they owned while living or your favourite photos of them. You may wish to do this on the day of their birth or the anniversary of their death – feel into what makes sense to you.

What other major events could you put in your annual witchy calendar? Life-changing stuff has happened to you, I'm willing to bet. Does any of it deserve to be commemorated with a ritual, no matter how small and simple? Maybe you once had a spiritual experience that shifted your world on its axis and you acknowledge that you were never the same afterwards. Maybe you overcame addiction and you'd like to recognize your strength in recovery with each year that passes. Maybe surviving an accident or illness made you stronger and you'd like to recognize how that has contributed to your ongoing life journey. Choose a relevant or random date to celebrate this so that such significance isn't overlooked.

Witches often end up having special dates associated with milestones in their practice, too. For instance, a witch may like to recognize the anniversary of their decision to start practising witchcraft. Or they could recognize the date that they chose to dedicate themselves to a specific deity (see pages 76–7 for more on working with deities). If you're new to the path, you won't yet have any annual occasions based on your witchy experiences, but try keeping a note of when you made big decisions or experienced big changes, in case you want to commemorate them later.

YOUR WITCHY CALENDAR

WRITE IT

◊ What thoughts and feelings does the word 'birthday' bring up in you? What about 'anniversary' or 'celebration'? Try delving into the associations which come to mind.

◊ What are the potential benefits of recognizing your own birthday in some kind of witchy context?

◊ Write a list of the important events in your life which could be factored into your witchy yearly cycle of celebration and commemoration.

TRY IT

◊ Consider any funerals, anniversaries or other commemorative events you have been to and decide what you thought was helpful and suitable. As you do this exercise, notice which elements of these events seem to resonate with you and which ones you didn't vibe with as much. This will guide you into how you would set up a memorial in a way that honours your outlook and personality.

Celebration of Heroes, Icons and Saints

Do you have favourite rock stars, poets, painters, composers, actors, spiritual teachers or philosophers who left a deep impression on your soul with their work before exiting planet Earth? How about sprinkling some days of honour into your witchy calendar to commemorate your faves on their birthdays? This could give you the opportunity to explore their work in a spiritual context, give thanks for what their legacy has given to you and maybe make contact with their spirit or energy (depending on whether that's a part of your belief structure). You don't have to keep your options open to only figures who've already passed on. Celebrate the birthday of a living hero, if you feel like it, taking time to appreciate their ideas or admire their actions while sitting in sacred space. You could even also send them a magickal token of your appreciation if you'd like to!

You may find that working with your heroes and favourite icon figures is useful for calling their qualities toward yourself so that you can deal with certain situations. You don't have to do this on a birthday, just do it whenever you feel like it (see pages 82–3 for more on this concept).

Witches who work with saints or other types of religious beings often observe their respective feast days, making offerings, saying prayers and blessings, and so on. Some figures, such as the Virgin Mary, have several different feast days representing different aspects of their story and qualities. Some deities from pre-Christian times still have feast days or periods when they are honoured. You can put these in your calendar if it feels right to do so. You can also choose feast days for beings who don't seem to have one or for beings of your own creation. (We'll delve into the exciting realm of constructing and communing with beings on pages 71–86.)

WRITE IT

◊ Who really inspires you and how might that inspiration be useful for you in your craft? Choose one to three figures to write about.

◊ Why might it be powerful and important to dedicate an entire ritual or day to a deity/being, focusing on their powers and their value in your life? What could the positive effects of this be?

TRY IT

◊ Take time to close your eyes and visualize the kind of vibe that you associate with a particular figure so that you can welcome that same type of vibe into yourself. Whenever I think of Frida Kahlo, for example, I feel the energies of passion, steadfastness, sensuality, bravery and unabashed authenticity. When I visualize that kind of energy signature surrounding me and entering my body and my consciousness, I find myself absorbing and using it to face my own challenges. Try it! (This works whether it's the person's birthday or not, so feel free to use the technique any time.) You may wish to change up the figures whose birthdays are observed in your yearly calendar, depending on the different vibes you want to bring into your life.

◊ Imagine that you yourself are a sacred being for whom a witch is having a feast day! What kind of ceremony/ritual/ occasion would they need to hold in order to reflect your qualities and powers? What kinds of food, music, colours etc should be present?

Mainstream and Non-witchy Occasions

Being a witch doesn't necessarily mean having to part with all the non-witchy stuff that characterizes the journey through the year in the society you inhabit. Many witches recognize Easter, Christmas and Halloween alongside their Wheel of the Year counterparts – Ostara, Winter Solstice and Samhain. As a witch, you don't have to give up any former religious or secular observances that brought meaning or fun to your life. However, you might decide to drop out of some completely because they don't resonate anymore, while keeping the ones that make you feel warm and fuzzy.

It is pretty usual for witches to compromise when it comes to the mainstream stuff. Many witchy peeps have loved ones who would be downhearted if they just bowed out of an occasion altogether. So a witch might choose to go to the Christmas dinner and gift exchange, for example, but skip out on the family church attendance. Witches who are still in the broom closet may feel pressured to involve themselves in events they don't resonate with in order to fit in sometimes. If you find yourself in this situation, you can do some witchy business in advance and afterwards to ensure that you feel centred and shielded throughout the experience (see page 165 for more on protection).

WRITE IT

◊ Describe the best feelings that you have about a non-witchy occasion you've celebrated, such as a religious observance or a cultural tradition.

◊ Also try writing about the worst feelings you had at such an event.

TRY IT

◊ Consider which non-witchy occasions genuinely mean something to you and try engaging in conversations with others about this. Discover what you have in common with others and what you disagree about.

Days of Awareness – Including Made-up Ones

There are plenty of national and international days of awareness to recognize, many of which are linked to specific organizations and movements that raise money for important causes. You can insert the initiatives you care about in your witchy calendar so you remember to take action on those days. You could perform a fizzy, high-vibe healing ritual for a cause you're passionate about, spread awareness on social media, make a donation or give your time to volunteer.

As a rebel witch you might just get the urge to sprinkle some totally random days into your calendar. They can be days dedicated to all kinds of things! Here are a few ideas:

- *A day to honour your favourite band:* You could play their music and watch their videos during a ritual to recognize the influence they've had on your life.
- *A day to honour a favourite film:* Invite the energy of a movie character you love and see what they have to tell you.
- *A day to honour your favourite TV series:* Watch in sacred space and note down the quotes which seem magickal and important to you, analyzing their meanings afterwards to see how they could offer guidance.
- *A day to honour an artist or style of art:* Tune into the power of the artist and/or style, calling it into your life and honouring its influence on you.

- *A day of silence for inner peace:* Let your peeps know you'll be silent all day and take time away from your phone, too.
- *Activism day:* Attend a protest or engage in some online activism, directing your intention toward justice and resolution.
- *Declutter-and-cleanse day:* Get the physical cleaning of your room or home out of the way first and then it's time to tidy energetically (see pages 95–8).
- *Witchy crafting day:* Try making potions, poppets or your own set of oracle cards (see pages 110–30 for more on witchy tools).
- *Astrology day:* Explore your natal chart and see how it's had an influence on your month/year so far. Or check out what astrologers have to say about your sign.
- *Inner child day:* Revisit your younger self, engaging in the activities they liked to enjoy and indulging in the treats, movies or books that they loved.
- *Divination day:* Break out your cards or your crystal ball, or do some scrying, to get answers to your burning questions. (Divination methods are explored on pages 189–93.)
- *Dress-up day:* Become one of your favourite characters for the entire day! You might even be daring enough to go out to the shops or out with friends, dressed up and in character.

Remember that you're building your own unique tradition. At first, your shiny new ideas might feel a bit silly or pointless. You may see the Sabbats and Esbats as the "real deal", because they're staples of the witchcraft world, whereas a day of channelling your favourite cartoon character in order to do spells might feel like it doesn't have the same power. But a witch's power comes from *personalizing* their processes. If you're not invested in what you're doing, it's not likely to work. Honouring the music, books, concepts etc that matter to you is so potent because it means that you're putting your signature onto each witchy act you carry out. Keep this in mind as you go along.

WRITE IT

◊ Make a list of the causes and issues that really matter
to you – the problems that keep you awake at night, the
shitty bits that really bother you most about reality.
Then find out if there are days of awareness for those
issues and which organizations support those causes. You
could then choose at least one day of awareness for your
witchy calendar.

◊ What could be the pros and cons of having some random
events of your choosing in your witchy calendar?

TRY IT

◊ When you've logged at least one day of awareness in your
calendar, close your eyes and begin to generate the feeling
of empowerment and positivity that comes when you
know you've done something useful for a good cause. Let
that feeling fill your body and change your perception of
your day, your place in the world and what is possible in
the future.

◊ Invent concepts for two to four celebratory days in your
witchy year. Consider including days to honour or interact
with the things you're really interested in learning about.

◊ Visualize yourself carrying out the events of these days.
What does it feel like to imagine them?

9

DIVINE AND OTHER NON-PHYSICAL BEINGS

There's a veritable avalanche of goodness to explore in this area, sugar plum! I'm feeling giddy as I'm writing about it. There's an abundance of beings to work with, and in this chapter we'll visit some of the key types. Although many witches happily follow the "matron and patron" model – working closely with a primary god and goddess, usually from an ancient civilization – you don't have to drop anchor there if you want to wade out into weirder waters. You could work with a rich and complex cast of different beings, fostering a unique relationship with each one. You may want to find deities to receive advice from and make offerings to regularly, while also looking to spend time with other deities/beings on a casual basis or explore interactions as they come up.

This section of the book deals with beings that do not have an earthly physical form. But just because they are disembodied doesn't mean they don't have an *appearance*. Some beings are widely agreed to look a certain way, whether you actually ever see them or not. In fact, many are depicted as human in their appearance, such as lots of the gods and goddesses we're familiar with. Others look more like animals or a combination of animal and human. Some look like shapes of textured and coloured energy or wobbling vibrations in the air. Some shift from one form to another. And some of the beings you encounter will never reveal an appearance to you – instead, they'll give you more of a vibe or emotion that you'll be able to tap into when they're close to you or giving you a message.

One thing I want to stress is that you're under no obligation to work with beings at all. If it's not your cup of tea, that's all good. You can work with the powers of nature's different elements and seasons, or with your sense of your own ability to make things happen. Working with beings is not mandatory and you can definitely have a high-powered practice without feeling the need to work with deities, spirits, fairies, servitors and the like. If you want to skip this entire section, go right ahead. But if you've been wanting to give yourself permission to consider working with beings (or open up to different kinds of beings), you might find some reassurance and inspiration here.

So why would a witch seek out a non-physical being? These are just some of the advantages:

- Assistance in magickal workings.
- Help with life's challenges.
- Protection and an ally on the path of life.
- Guidance and wisdom from beyond the earthly realm.
- Mentorship and inspiration.
- Deep lessons from an epic teacher.
- Confirmation that working with non-physical beings actually works.
- Keeping life interesting and satisfying your curiosity!

Although I'm always thrilled by the concept of choice when working with beings, it's worth noting that instead of choosing, you may *be chosen*. You could be minding your own business one day when all of a sudden you are contacted by a disembodied being offering you a message or invitation to interact. The way this happens varies. One witch may find they're visited in a dream or meditation by the same being many times, eventually deciding to make that being into a permanent fixture.

MAKE IT HAPPEN

Another may have a strong feeling that a being they're researching is resonating with them; that feeling may grow stronger and turn into a kind of "calling". For others, a deity or being makes themselves known in a single "power move", entering dramatically and immediately grabbing the witch's attention, maybe via a strong sign, a potent dream/vision or a compelling sense of presence.

But don't feel intimidated or disappointed if you're not chosen in one of these ways. You can simply begin a sincere search for beings to work with by declaring yourself open to any positive interactions. You might do this by conducting a ritual that symbolizes your readiness and desire to connect with beings, provided that such connections would be useful and positive for you. You can then be intrigued to see what kinds of messages and interactions come through. If you have a particular being in mind, you can go ahead and start the conversation, welcoming them to get back to you if they feel inclined to do so.

In my case, I knew I really wanted to be connected to Hel, the Norse goddess of death and the underworld. Rather than waiting for her to give me a wink and a nod, I instead researched everything I could get my hands on about her, made images of her with paint and collage, wrote about her and asked her to visit me in dreams or send me signs. It was a slow start but over the course of time I did experience interactions and the connection strengthened. Don't let anyone tell you that you have to wait on the sidelines until a being picks you and asks you to dance. You are allowed to be bold. You are allowed to make the first move, especially if you know which appeals to you. Why not reach out and make friends if you can envision a thriving connection? Just remember to be patient. These kinds of experiences can come on slowly. You may need to keep reiterating your interest in connecting while also developing your path in other ways.

There are so many shades of belief around what is actually happening when you connect with a non-physical being. Some peeps reckon that disembodied beings such as gods and spirit guides exist on other planes beyond the material one that we inhabit, and that it's possible to

DIVINE AND OTHER NON-PHYSICAL BEINGS

send and receive messages to and from them. Others believe that the beings are not on another plane but born of the human imagination, fed by the energy of our focus as we develop stories around them and invest belief in them, allowing them to achieve some form of separate existence. There are those who believe that all the non-physical beings they might encounter are different aspects of the same thing – slices of divinity, essentially. Each being is like a piece of a jigsaw, holding within it the essence of the complete puzzle while only ever being one part of it. Other witches believe each being has its own separate energy and consciousness, not part of one big puzzle but a puzzle in its own right. Of course, there's also a belief that non-physical beings are all just elaborate make-believe and a distraction from "real life". (Yes, even witches themselves can choose to believe that if they wish, and many do. In fact, my belief is somewhat connected to this last theory, in the sense that we don't really know what the truth is, so it may as well be that!)

You might not be sure what you believe about this stuff and yet still find yourself drawn to working with a deity, guide or other disembodied personality. Maybe you feel silly about your interest in beings, but you can't shake the feeling that it would be cool to have them in your life. It's OK to answer your own questions as you take the journey. Sometimes that's the only way to do it. You may want to try working with a non-physical being simply for shits 'n' giggles, just to see what happens. You can learn and strengthen so much when you do something that takes you off the beaten track and challenges your sense of what's possible. It's easy to obstruct your own path by insisting that you need to have your reasons all worked out before you add something to your practice. You could stand on the sidelines *for ever*, trying to figure out if you believe that it's possible for you to interact with non-physical beings, but you'll only truly know by trying it out for yourself.

Many witches work with big hitters from the world of deity. Maybe you've heard of Thor and Odin from Norse mythology, for example, or Zeus and Hades from Greek mythology? Perhaps goddesses such as Aphrodite, Isis, Cerridwen and Kali ring a bell? (From the Greek, Egyptian, Celtic and Hindu pantheons respectively.) Those are some well-known examples, although many witches work with lesser-known deities who can be just as powerful but don't have as much modern-day cultural clout. If you're not super-clued-up on deities, that's OK! It might become an area of deep interest for you and you may find yourself discovering deities from different eras and civilizations as you do research. It can be fascinating to learn about mythological and religious figures that you'd never heard of. Some witches do venerate and work with the Christian God, Jesus, the Virgin Mary, the saints – even Satan. This is something that can raise eyebrows both within and outside the witchy community, but for the witches engaged with those beings, it works and makes sense.

WRITE IT

◊ What do the following words and phrases make you think and feel, and why?: "Deity", "God", "Goddess", "worship", "prayer", "divine", "omnipresent", "non-physical", "non-human", "disembodied".

◊ What do you consider to be some of the pros and cons of working with non-physical beings? You might want to consider this from your own point of view, but also in broader terms, for other people too.

TRY IT

◊ Invent your own pantheon! What would your water deity be like and why? What about the deities/beings associated with war, art, justice, childbirth and so on? You could use pre-existing pantheons for inspiration, reworking each of the deities in your imagination so they are connected more closely to your passions and experiences. For example, perhaps a war god would be a punk rock singer in your personal pantheon, belting out songs about corruption and inequality. Your deity of justice could be a graffiti artist with a political message. You might want non-human deities, like a gigantic neon pink starfish as your queen of the sea or a nature god fashioned from an enveloping green mist. Let this be an ongoing brainstorm – a creative project that allows you to explore your spiritual perspectives. You don't need to actively work with the invented pantheon if you don't want to. But you could!

Different Types of Non-physical Beings

Let's explore some of the beings that you can consider bringing into your practice:

Ancient deities

Divine non-physical beings who rule or influence different aspects of earthly reality can have a profound effect on your witchcraft and on your life overall. There are various pantheons of divine beings to explore, and you'll notice that they're peppered with so many of the same themes and energies. For instance, deities of war with various names, attributes and characteristics are present in mythologies from all over the world. They are each connected to the same universal theme, but they each have a unique name, appearance and set of experiences. It's the same with deities connected to beauty, love, death, mischief, destruction, the forest, the home ...

Some of these deities had opulent temples built in their honour, which once were filled with devotees leaving offerings. Do you have any fond memories of doing a school project about the religious beliefs of an ancient civilization (even if school was tough for you and you felt like an outsider!)? I remember learning about Athena for the first time and feeling like my whole body was suddenly covered in fairy lights. It was exhilarating to look at images of this ancient Greek goddess of wisdom, and I felt the same when classes about the ancient Egyptians led me to focus on Isis, Osiris and Bast. You may feel called to a specific deity who's been holding your interest and popping into your mind for years. Or you might notice that you're attracted to various deities aligned with the same theme; perhaps you feel a pull toward death deities, or deities ruling fertility or those associated with water or hunting.

Spirit guides

The term "spirit guide" is actually pretty broad and could include other categories in this list: they are essentially non-physical beings who offer guidance or protection to you. Your deceased auntie might be one of your spirit guides. Another might be in the form of an angel, or a blue-green sparkling energy who shows up to offer reassurance, or a forest spirit who occupies your favourite tree or a shimmering octopus with wings who appears sometimes in your daydreams. There are tons of possibilities. Some people have one spirit guide – others have an army of them. You may know some of your spirit guides very well after many regular interactions, while others visit less often and play a more minor role in your life. Sometimes the guidance your spirit guide offers is not what you were hoping for and you can certainly choose to ignore it, but the consequences of that decision can be messy! You might find guides who regularly visit to be more trusted or their messages easier to understand, but it's different for everyone.

Ghosts/spirits

Apparitions of the dead sometimes just appear to people (literally or energetically) and don't necessarily have anything to say. But witches often find that they can chat with ghosts or receive offers of information from them. You can use the word "spirit" in place of "ghost", and many do. It tends to be common to say "spirit" if you're talking about someone you knew before they passed or who was a blood ancestor, whereas "ghost" is usually reserved to describe the presence of a deceased person you're not familiar with. Ghosts may visit because they know that a witch is more likely to accurately translate or use their messages. Spirits of friends or ancestors turn up due to the emotional and/or blood connection there, and you may actually call them in yourself – many witches like to work with their deceased relatives.

Animal allies/guides

If you're particularly connected to the characteristics and symbolism of a specific animal, you can bring the imagery of that animal into your practice and make it sacred to you. You may decide that you'll learn from its behaviours and call upon its strengths and abilities in your times of need. Seeing that particular animal in your dreams and visions, or at significant times in your waking life, could be interpreted as an important message. Any folktales, myths, songs or artworks containing the animal will obviously then become significant, too. You can choose your animal allies and guides or find that they choose you. (Insects also count!)

Elementals

The elements of earth, air, fire and water are widely considered to be sacred in witchcraft. Elementals are beings associated with the power of these four elements. They live in and around locations such as trees, rivers, flower beds, lakes, forests, woodlands, groves, meadows – you get the picture. Lots of witches who work with elementals tend to recognize four principle types: gnomes (for earth), undines (for water), sylphs (for air) and salamanders (for fire). If you feel drawn to the idea that there are attending spirits at natural sites, then researching these four types of elementals could be a good jumping-off point. Elementals may also be known as nymphs, and there are many types of nymph related to different places in the natural world. However, you may find that pre-existing ideas about elementals only tell parts of the story. Having your own experiences with them will help you to see that there can be a lot more to it.

Other mythical/fairytale creatures

Maybe you're drawn to vampires, dragons, unicorns, fairies, goblins, harpies, mermaids, pixies, werewolves or zombies. Maybe you're interested in a specific creature, such as the Firebird from Slavic folklore or the Minotaur who roams the labyrinth in the ancient Greek myth. If you have a strong instinct that you want to work with a specific type of non-physical creature, research into the original legends that describe it will add context and richness to your understanding. You get to consider what the various beings from myth and folklore symbolize for you and how they might help you with your endeavours or teach you something powerful. Remember, no one else gets to tell you how you ought to think of certain beings or their role in your world. You may see a certain type of creature quite differently to another witch's perspective – and that's OK.

Imaginary friends

As a kid, were you accompanied by an inspiring, encouraging companion, invisible to everyone but you? Were the adults (and perhaps other children) around you regaled with tales of your faithful friend? Maybe they got you into trouble, or kept you out of it? This character can make an epic reappearance in your craft. Why not? You already have a strong sense of who they are and how they can help you, so it might make total sense to shake them awake inside your psyche and let them play a powerful role in your magickal workings and other witchiness. If your imaginary friend was an animated stuffed animal or other object that's no longer in your possession, it's still all good. If you really want to, you can summon the being's essential nature without the body it once inhabited. Just bring the toy to mind, remembering its appearance and texture, and how it made you feel when you held it and played with it.

DIVINE AND OTHER NON-PHYSICAL BEINGS

Fictional characters from films, books, TV series and cartoons

The characters we seriously vibed with during childhood and adolescence can make riveting travel companions on the witchy journey, and I really can't overstate that! Fictional characters shape who we become, offering texture and depth to our sense of ethics, identity and potential. There's so much of ourselves that we didn't get from our parents or from the immediate circumstances of our upbringing; instead, we got it from the fictional characters we loved, who shepherded and mentored us in ways we would otherwise have been deprived of. This generosity from the fictional realm extends into adulthood, turning our thoughts on their axis and adding to our sense of what is possible for the rest of our lives until death. The love you feel for the characters that have made an impact on you translates into power that can be used for spellcraft and ritual. You can call on those characters, take on their mentalities and evoke their energies when needed. Some characters may become ongoing symbols of what you want to achieve in your craft or the kind of practitioner you want to remind yourself to be.

Servitors

Why should you always have to choose from what's already out there, honey bee? Maybe you want magickal backup but feel there's no pre-existing deity, fictional character or mythical creature that flicks your switch. If you're looking for a being to help you with something specific, you can take matters into your own witchy hands. Servitors are designed to carry out set tasks. They can spring into action whenever you're having issues in a particular area – money, home, work or love life, for example. You choose the servitor's name, appearance and what it will help you with. You can devise a way to summon it and send it away again. Some servitors are with you for life, but some may be more temporary and can be given a lifespan. For example, maybe you only need a servitor to help you with wedding planning and wedding day nerves, after which it will "disperse" having done its job.

MAKE IT HAPPEN

Other entities and thoughtforms of your own creation

Aside from making servitors to help you with magickal and mundane stuff, you may also want to consider creating your own deities or guides to accompany you on your journey. After all, you might not feel that any pre-existing being quite fits with your needs or represents who you are as a person, so inventing a being from the sacred realm of your own imagination will mean it's as powerful as possible. A rebel witch knows that what comes from their own imagination and passion often stands a high chance of creating results and being deeply satisfactory. Rather than disempowering yourself by being convinced that your own inventions must mean less than what's out there already, you can decide that a deity or guide that's constructed using bits and pieces of your own psyche is definitely going to be super-high-powered. Perhaps you'd like a deity with a personal connection to the small town you live in, or a deity who's trans or non-binary, or a deity who shapeshifts to look like all your favourite film stars ... If what you want isn't out there, you can birth it from your imagination.

Archetypes

In films and books you can recognize certain types of characters: the Victim, the Hero, the Villain, the Mentor, the Chosen One, the Loveable Rogue, the Gentle Giant, the Damsel-in-Distress, the Loner, the Sage ... All these roles are archetypes: the different parts we play as human beings – our mental and emotional blueprints. We interact with these roles in different ways, and when it comes to archetypes, one witch's trash can certainly be another witch's treasure. Consider the archetypes you feel most moved and inspired by. You might want to create a collection of images that tap you into a key archetype's power, perhaps including images of characters you love that portray that archetype or just leaning into imagery that visually describes the archetype's energy.

Heroes and icons

I personally draw massive magickal power and spiritual inspiration from certain deceased musicians, especially Jimi Hendrix, Freddie Mercury, Leonard Cohen and Kurt Cobain. There are images of all these men in my apartment and I see them as guiding forces in their own ways. There are also writers, artists and activists I could name whose birthdays I like to recognize or whose quotes and achievements I return to when I'm feeling lost. I've made devotional candles featuring the faces of iconic people whose work is a guiding light for me. You can bring figures of inspiration into your practice, even if they are no longer physically living. You may not necessarily feel able to work with them in the same way as deities, but you may notice the positive and empowering effect they have on you and count it as a spiritual tool.

––––––––

Here's a list of possibilities to try when connecting with a non-physical being. You could:

- Write devotional poetry, stories or songs or choreograph a dance in honour of the being.
- Make jewellery or other crafts in honour of them.
- Make toasts to them when having a drink.
- Speak to them in the morning and before bed, or at some other set times.
- Identify certain signs that represent the presence of the being, knowing that when these signs show up, your being is close or has a message for you.
- Observe a yearly feast day for them.
- Dedicate a specific lunar phase or day of the month to them.
- Create a shrine to them or dedicate a section of your altar to them.
- Keep a notebook that is just for reflections about them, signs you received from them, etc. Try channelled writing, asking the being to write through you.

- Evoke the energy of the being, perhaps by dressing up as them or playing appropriate music, and then allow the vibe of the being to enter you in order to understand them more fully.
- Overcome your fears and challenges in their honour and dedicate your victories to them.
- Do all kinds of things in their name and/or honour, such as working out, decluttering your space or doing volunteer work.
- Create a specific playlist to honour/represent them and play it when you want them to be close to you or give you guidance.
- Pray to them for help with solving issues and finding answers.
- Continue your study of all the myths and stories associated with them, historical discoveries related to them and the civilization they come from, etc.
- Join a special interest group dedicated to talking about them.
- Make offerings to them.

When it comes to offerings, you can figure out what is appropriate. With the more established deities, there's a consensus around what kinds of offerings they appreciate best, and you can research that if you want to see what the deal is. But naturally, the rebel witch way is one of feeling into what clicks with you as an individual practitioner, and your relationship with a deity isn't necessarily going to match up uniformly with someone else's, so your offerings may look different to theirs. Sometimes a deity may inspire you to give an unexpected offering. Feel free to just go with it. If you get an urge to pick up a feather or stone because you feel your deity would like it placed on the altar for them, go for it. Or you might find something in a shop that you feel will make a good offering. You can also give parts of your own meals and drinks as offerings when the fancy takes you. Of course, with other beings – including ones of your own invention – there's no consensus around offerings, which is actually really fun. See what your intuition and imagination cook up as potential offerings and, of course, you may find that your being tells you what they like anyway. A witch's astral army can be big hint-droppers.

My main working deity, Hel the Norse death goddess, indicated to me that I should offer her my sweat. In other words, she urged me to be more consistent with my exercise regime and consider each workout to be an offering to her. This was a great message to receive because it boosted my activity level as well as giving me a way to connect with divinity without separating the mystical from the mundane. When you see gardening, baking, exercising, walking the dog, decluttering, paying bills, breastfeeding or doing the school run to be valid ways of connecting with a deity, you open up the practice of communion so that it's 24/7 rather than being confined to devotionals at the altar.

You can choose to dedicate yourself to a being, performing a ritual to symbolize your commitment to ongoing work with them. Dedicating yourself to a being shows how seriously you take the connection. It also gives you a chance to outline the terms of the relationship. For instance, your dedication ritual could be a time for you to vow that you'll make offerings or carry out devotionals to the being regularly, or that you'll honour them by emulating their characteristics, learning from their myths, etc. Dedication to a being usually feels like a big deal, so it may depend on how long the relationship has lasted. There's no rush to dedicate, and you might choose not to do it at all. It's kind of like marriage in that way! (If you want to figure out a good way to do a dedication ritual, see pages 172–3.)

Many witches are dedicated to more than one being, so don't worry about feeling the need to choose one above others that you may work with. But if you feel inclined toward total exclusively to one being in your practice, I'd say go with that flow. For some witches, being in one committed divine relationship is more than enough eventfulness without adding more cosmic connections into the equation. If you work with numerous beings, you may find that some have a recurring role, while others only make cameo appearances. A goddess or spirit guide could be in your life for decades, while another might come along with one key piece of information and then leave the scene. You may choose to invest more emotion and focus in the connections that over time prove themselves to be central to you, and that may involve dedicating yourself to a being – or several.

Remember, any non-physical beings that you work with are subject to change as your journey progresses. You may feel that a being you used to

MAKE IT HAPPEN

see in your dreams, connect with in ritual or even dedicated yourself to and worked with regularly, will stop making themselves available to you. They will become distant until they eventually seem to have disappeared. Not all beings will remain with you for the rest of your life, no matter how vital your connection with them felt at one point. To be honest, this can be saddening. For lots of witches, the feeling of drifting apart from a being with whom they used to work closely feels gloomy. Why does this even happen? Well, why does any relationship end? Needs change, interests change or life just changes you. Other things feel more shiny, more healthy, less strenuous, more relevant. You may simply need to be alone for a while. There may be an issue with miscommunication, growing at different rates, pulling in different directions or just feeling like things have become monotonous. Sometimes you've simply learned everything you can from the connection.

Personally, I believe it's OK for a being to enter a witch's life for a season rather than a lifetime. Some beings have a certain bag of tricks to deliver to you, offering life lessons and skills that you needed at the time, only to retreat once their work is done. Sometimes, when a being leaves, it's understood and feels like a mutually chosen goodbye. But sometimes it's like a heartbreak, and if that happens, it will take time to heal, just as it does when a beloved human walks out of your life. You may feel that you've left the door open emotionally for the being to return, and that may well happen. But try to direct your attention toward other parts of your practice, rather than pining too long for what's been and gone.

Keep in mind that it's possible to push too hard for beings to show up in your life. If working with a disembodied intelligence seems like a super-attractive concept, then you might fixate on it and feel disillusioned if that experience doesn't arrive. You may also risk overlooking other potentially fizzy parts of the witchcraft practice. If you're not getting results when calling a being into your witchy world, try stepping back and focusing your attention on other things for a while. It's sort of like the old saying, "A watched pot never boils". A tense, fixated desire for beings to appear can create delay in their arrival. Try to be a bit less adamant and enjoy other parts of the craft.

DIVINE AND OTHER NON-PHYSICAL BEINGS

WRITE IT

◊ What are your plans for the next three to six months when it comes to working with disembodied beings, and why?

TRY IT

◊ If you're curious about working with beings but still at the beginning of your explorations, start doing some research into at least one existing deity or mythical being that interests you. There's no need to open up a line of communication with this being at first. Just enjoy the habit of researching different non-physical intelligences.

◊ Do you already work with beings? Try this. Consider the ways in which you have instigated greater closeness with fellow human beings such as co-workers, friends and family members. What do you notice about your own particular ways of inviting more closeness with others and sustaining it once it's been built? See how many of those techniques for getting closer to humans can be used in your mission to get closer to other beings. Skills for building closeness are transferable from human bonds to bonds with non-physical intelligences.

◊ Take a look online at what witches have to say about the beings they work with. In particular, what do you notice about the benefits witches seem to receive from working with a being?

SPIRITUAL HYGIENE: CLEANSING ENERGY AND CREATING SACRED SPACE

Let's get into the topic of energy and how to cleanse, direct, raise and hold it in a way that feels right for you. I'm going to have to go a bit hippie on you now ... When I say "energy", I'm referring to "the vibes, man". Have you ever sensed that two people in a room you've just entered are in a mood with each other somehow, even if there's no obvious signs that there's been an altercation? Ever gotten a shiver up the spine on a tour around a historical site where a lot of unpleasant things took place? Have you been in a situation when you've sensed you're safe and the energy has gone from volatile to stable – or vice versa? Have you sometimes just felt that the atmosphere has shifted and that you need to respond accordingly? Those were all times when you were reading the energy – catching the vibes.

Reading and assessing the energies around you is something you may often do in your everyday life without even noticing. If someone asked you to explain why you decided to leave a party, change your mind about pursuing an opportunity or take a different route on your usual hiking trail, maybe you wouldn't always have been able to clarify your reasons. You just acted on instinct, feeling, *vibes*. Some people assess the energy of a location unconsciously. For witches, it's usually very intentional. Being able to feel and read the energy of a location, person or object is a pretty common thing for witchy types. Many of us can sense crappy or low vibes, reacting to our instincts before anything has obviously changed in the external world. This splendidly spooky behaviour can sometimes be noticed by people around you. They'll ask, "How the hell did you know that was going to happen?", or they'll note that you managed to avoid delay, inconvenience or danger by making an instinctive decision. But if that's not your experience, don't worry. You can still totally be a witch. Our skillsets and perspectives are all different. It's OK to be a witch who relies more on external information and objective fact. Remember that you also don't have to be in one camp or the other; there's a whole spectrum of ability in energy-reading and fact-finding.

Lots of witchy resources encourage you to cleanse your energy before workings and then ground your energy afterwards. They also urge you to cleanse homes before you move into them, cleanse your witchy tools and cleanse *yourself*. You'll also find that most resources strongly advise you to create sacred space before performing rituals and spells. Sacred space is a witch's barrier of defence. It locks your desired energy and atmosphere and leaves anything else out in the cold. These acts are encouraged to increase your safety and make your experiences positive. Such practices can definitely hold power, but let's drop the dogma that's built up around them. Figure out how *you* feel about "energy" and how to manage it. Invite yourself to question how often such energy-hygiene practices are actually needed. Are they non-negotiable? Are they always relevant? Do they always need to be carried out in the same old ways? Do you sometimes feel pressured into cleansing even when you don't feel that it's needed?

I take my energy-hygiene decisions on a case-by-case basis, preferring to feel out each situation to decide what's necessary rather than expending tons of effort where I may not need to. For example, when I first moved into the home I currently rent, I got a nice, fluffy high vibe from the moment I turned the key in the lock – I didn't sense anything uncool. I went upstairs and the previous occupant had left a sprig of lavender for me on the windowsill alongside a quote from the Dalai Lama about being in the moment, which deepened my sense that the person who'd just moved out didn't leave any energetic muck for me to deal with. In fact, it was the opposite – the energy she *did* leave was pleasing to me and I got the feeling it would merge well with my own. So, while I cleaned the surfaces and vacuumed before unpacking my belongings, I didn't give the space any *energetic* cleansing attention because I personally felt absolutely fine about not doing so. (I can't say as much for the place I lived in beforehand – an apartment full of weird tension and haphazard energy. It took *two* sound energy-cleansing sessions and a house blessing before I'd move my stuff in!)

Before doing any energy work, ask yourself:

- Does this work feel necessary?
- Will this work be truly helpful?
- What is the pre-existing energy actually like and could it be useful to me in some way?
- Is it important to let the energy remain as it is so that I can learn from it and wait for it to change organically?
- Do I just need to leave rather than worrying about trying to shift the energy?

Cleansing Yourself

Let's say something just feels energetically "off" or unpleasant. The energy doesn't seem to be flowing nicely, the vibes feel a bit dense or sticky somehow. It could be because there are stacks of disorganized papers and books around, clothes and towels on the floor, random clutter on the surfaces. But even if you do the physical tidying, there could still be a feeling of misalignment. Maybe that's due to a crappy energy leftover from something that happened the day before – something lingering that needs to be cleared. You may not be able to figure out if it's your *own* vibe that needs adjustment or something in your surroundings that needs to be booted out, in which case it might help if you cleanse yourself first and then work on the space (if indeed you still feel the need). Let's take a look at some potential reasons for deciding to cleanse your own energy:

- You just spent time in a tense or unpleasant environment and you're still feeling that vibe around you even after leaving the location.
- You've had an argument and your energy feels totally off as a result.
- You've been detecting and absorbing other people's high-intensity emotions during the day.
- You feel that someone else is directing their malice or judgement toward you and you're absorbing whatever they're sending your way.
- You're undergoing medical treatment that leaves you feeling disconnected or misaligned.
- You're preparing for a challenging situation ahead, such as a tense work meeting, a difficult personal call, a competitive sports game or a big party, and you want your energy to be strong, gathered and focused going into it.
- You find that cleansing your energy makes you feel more stable and helps your mental and emotional wellbeing.

What does it mean for you to cleanse your own energy? What would it look like to positively change the vibe that you're giving off from your own body and mind? Let's face it, the most helpful answers to these questions are probably going to rely on your personal insights into your own needs and preferences. The less generic, the better. But you can also try some of the methods commonly used by spiritual peeps to cleanse their aura (which is the distinctive, individual energy generated by each person, place and object):

- Imagine yourself breathing in warmth and positivity and then exhaling stress, heaviness etc, for five to ten minutes.

MAKE IT HAPPEN

- Visualize a protective bubble around you in a colour of your choice, which pushes out any interfering energies and puts your own energy in a positive and protected state.
- Do a body-scan meditation to take compassion and focus to any aches or tension and end up feeling more relaxed and connected.
- Take a bath or shower with the water acting as a symbol of cleansing and rejuvenation, washing away what's not wanted.

Now, just because we're going for the rebel witch perspective doesn't mean that the tried 'n' tested techniques are to be entirely sniffed at. On the contrary, it wouldn't be very pro-rebellion of me to advise you against using something that could work well for you just because it's a time-honoured tradition. But consider how completely unique your energy is and the unfiltered, intimate connection you have with it. That shit's powerful. So, when something's ungroovy in your aura, it'll respond to a carefully constructed toolkit. Any of the techniques above could help – and there's lots of other suggestions out there. Pop them into the kit, for sure, customize them to your needs, and then go on a journey to consider exactly how your energy could be adjusted and cleansed in a way that best suits you.

Here are some other ideas:

- Maybe you could visualize being surrounded by a group of your favourite superheroes, or cartoon or computer-game characters as they help you battle the badness in your energy field and get it back to its best.
- The bubble of protective light could be seen as the bubble that Glinda the Good Witch uses as her mode of transport in *The Wizard of Oz* (that's one of my personal favourites, seriously – that bubble just feels so sturdy!).
- Declare one particular song as your "energy-cleanse bop" – it's the one you play when you really need to get back to yourself. If the choice is too tough, make an energy-cleanse playlist.
- Pop a spell onto a piece of food that you keep for when you're feeling off, to help you get back to high vibes in a hurry.

SPIRITUAL HYGIENE

You'll need something long-life for this, such as a piece of confectionary or some seeds or nuts. (See Chapter 13 for more on spellcraft.)

- Have a special item of clothing or an accessory that has been activated to adjust your energy when it's imbalanced. Only wear the item when your energy is off – its job is to get you back to normal.

- Visit an energy-stash location in your imagination. This is a place where you'll keep bottles of distilled "self" for when you're feeling out of sorts. I have an altar in my imagination and there's a big fancy glass bottle of cleansing juice there for when I know my energy is all kinds of wrong. (I shake well before ingesting!)

- Design a dance routine or make up a song that clicks you back into selfhood, pronto.

- Imagine the low energy as an irritated goblin creature, rattling a cage inside of you. Hold your breath for as long as possible, focusing on how much you wanna release the little pest! Then, when you can hold your breath no longer and the high impact of that massive exhalation finally comes, see the goblin popping out of your mouth – and then kick it into the far distance for good measure.

- Call on your energy-clean-up servitor. This is a being you'll activate when you need a good sweep and clear out of your vibration. Maybe this servitor looks like a Barbie doll in a French maid's outfit. Maybe it's a guard dog that chases the bad vibes down the street with a deep growl (before cuddling up to you, obviously). Maybe it's a lovely cloud of lemon-scented smoke that sucks up the badness and leaves you feeling fresh.

- Keep a locked box into which you feed your low vibes and nasty feelings when you need to offload them. Once in a while, take the box to the edge of a cliff or body of water, or simply into the bathroom, to release its ungroovy contents out into the beyond or, you know, literally down the toilet (you can totally call it your bog box!).

- Into BDSM/kink? There could be so many ways to command and expel energy using themes and imagery from your particular part of that world. Could you assert dominance over your energy field, making it follow your detailed instructions and ultimately training it to improve? Or perhaps you know that engaging in thoughts about your kink tends to shift your energy in a positive direction, so use that to your advantage where possible.

I encourage lots of brainstorming around this. Go deep into what it means to get back to yourself. Remember that once your energy is back where it needs to be, you'll want to keep it locked. That can sometimes be a matter of focus and practice that then becomes a habit as time goes on. When I worked in an office, I used to get my aura together in the morning but end up feeling defeated by mid-afternoon, knowing that I'd allowed other people's energies to mess with my own. I always felt it should be possible to hold my own vibration while interacting with colleagues whose vibes were in a very different place, but I couldn't figure out exactly how to do it. Eventually I realized that, for me, it was just about practice. I took each day as an exciting opportunity to see if I could hold my energy for longer and with less effort, and the results were pretty astounding. (Maybe you're reading this and not really tapping into what I'm saying – and that's OK. The "energy stuff" won't resonate with everyone and just because it's a common experience doesn't mean it's a prerequisite for being a witch.)

A gentle reminder, poptart: It's possible to overdo the whole energy-cleansing thing, for sure. Sometimes we just need to be in our discomfort. It can be tough to deal with situations in your personal life as well as processing world events and trying to figure out how you fit into the overwhelming circus of it all. Energy cleansing is about shrugging off what's not useful, bringing yourself back to centre, back to focus – hitting a healthy reset button. It becomes harmful when we decide that all we need when we're feeling uncomfortable and sad is to cleanse it away. Pain and sadness are not a mistake in and of itself – they're a part of life, just like pleasure and happiness. If you find yourself experiencing more of the bad stuff than you can handle, energy cleanses are only part of a much bigger system of resources that I hope you'll feel empowered to reach out for. Talk to someone you can trust, look up appropriate helplines, make a doctor's appointment – take actions to bring support into your life rather than suffering alone.

SPIRITUAL HYGIENE

WRITE IT

◊ What does it mean to have an "energy"? What about shifting your energy? Holding your energy? What do these terms mean to you? Try using specific examples from your life in your exploration if possible.

◊ Reflect on a time when you were positively impacted by someone's energy (without them having to say or do anything).

◊ Then reflect on a time when you felt negatively impacted by someone's energy.

◊ What are the key mistakes and/or misunderstandings that you think people have about their energy and other people's?

TRY IT

◊ Notice the way in which you read/perceive the energy of the next three people you encounter.

◊ Practise developing confidence in the idea that you can hold your energy as you want it to be, locking or securing it so it's not easily affected by other powerful energies around you. For instance, when you sense tension, confusion or sadness in people around you, focus for a few moments on sending strength and intention to your energy so that it remains unchanged rather than being altered by the energies of others. This may take concentration at first, but it's likely that you'll eventually be able to do it easily while thinking and talking about other things. I assess and lock my energy every time I sense something ungroovy – it's second nature these days.

◊ Ask other people what they think about the concept of having an "energy" and being able to shift it and lock it. How do their opinions on this matter make you feel? How do their views affect your own perspective on this, if at all?

Cleansing Locations

When you choose to cleanse a room or an entire home, you may find that you need a decent amount of energy for the process. Make sure you're well rested and you've eaten something healthy 'n' helpful before doing this work. (Bananas and walnuts are my personal go-to, and a big bowl of pasta afterwards is a winner for me – I'm usually famished once I'm done.) Then decide on your role in the cleansing. Are you there to remove some low vibes that have collected in the space? Maybe you feel an energetic presence that shouldn't be there? If so, you might want to do a banishing spell (see pages 162–3) alongside your cleansing work. It's not always necessary, though. Lean into how you feel.

Perhaps there's an energy you'd like to bestow on the space? Are you going to be extending your own energy signature to it, because you want the space to be an energetic extension of the energy you're currently holding? If so, then it's about sending your vibration into the space – not in a way that *takes* it from you, but in more of a magickal "copy and paste" action. This means you can send your energy under the beds, inside the cupboards etc while still holding onto it yourself. This might sound difficult, but honestly it's not that different from being able to cheer someone up rather than feeling brought down by them. You can give a person your positive or calming energy without depleting your own, and it's the same with physical spaces.

But maybe you want the space to have a completely different energy. You can cleanse a space's pre-existing energy and replace it with whatever energy you like. It's normal to want a home office to have a different energetic feel to the bedroom, for example. As a witch, you may be asked to cleanse someone else's space, and they may request a calm, steady energy, a deeply relaxed energy or a strongly protective energy, depending on what's required.

One good way to bring a particular energy into a space during cleansing is to visualize something that conjures it up. Maybe you'd like a place to have the vibe of Stonehenge, an austere Tibetan monastery, your childhood holiday home, a charming picnic with a hamper and a bottle of Champagne, or a picturesque coast. If you struggle to hold such a concept in your mind while shifting the energy of the space, then use a recording of Tibetan chanting or waves lapping on the seashore, or whatever's associated with what you want to get across. If you're re-creating an energy from a memory of a place you've been, look at an image of that place for a long time before sending the associated energy into the space to be fixed there. If you want to come up with a concept for the energy, try making a mood/vision board on Pinterest, or the old-fashioned way – with paper, scissors and glue. Let the images help you conjure up the vibe you'd like the space to have.

Here are some more good options for cleansing a space and instating a new energy. You can do any of these things either physically or in your mind, or use a combination of mental and physical approaches – and, of course, feel free to tweak the suggestions or go entirely your own way if that suits you better:

- Light a candle (or use a lighter) dedicated to good intentions and positive energy for the space. Move around each room (either literally or using the power of your mind), shining the candle/lighter into each area of the space.
- Use smoke from incense, passing it through each part of the space, knowing that it carries your desired energy around the whole location.

MAKE IT HAPPEN

- Talk to the space, gently welcoming it to come into alignment with the energy you're introducing it to. Celebrate the space by giving it words of love and telling it what your intentions are for it.
- Tell a story of the future of the space, letting your imagination be filled with all that the space will be used for and all that you will experience within it. As you think/speak the story, visualize it coming true within the space.
- Call in the beings that you work with and ask them to help you fix the desired energy in the space and chase away any crappy vibes. If you have specifically sensed negative energy or an unpleasant vibe, ask the beings to help you eject it.
- Use sound to cleanse the space – chimes, bells, rattles and all kinds of musical instruments (including your own voice) can be highly effective tools. A portable speaker blasting your favourite music is always a good shout!
- Enchant the paint that will cover the walls of the space, putting spells of positivity and joy onto the furniture and breathe life into the posters of rock stars who will watch over you like guardians on the walls (see Chapter 13 for more on spells).
- Drop herbs and dried fruits, leaves or flowers of your choice mixed with salt around the space, maybe going into the corners and onto places of significance, to promote protection and strength to hold the energy under pressure. You can also use oils and tinctures for this, made by yourself or another witch.
- If you feel an unpleasant energy is hanging around, consider chasing it off by confronting it with something unpleasant. If you can find a compilation of yowling and fighting cats on the internet, that might be effective – I love cats but that sound does grate!
- Leave an open box in the centre of the space and command any negative energies/entities living there to get into the box and then dissolve or eat themselves or turn themselves into pleasant, high-vibe energies instead. This may take some time – you may want to repeat the command and sense that it is being heeded

before shutting the box. (It doesn't have to be a physical box – you can visualize one.)

Once the space has been cleansed and you've given it the intended energy, you might want to bless the place as a whole. I like to think of a blessing as kind of similar to a baby-naming ceremony. It's a way to recognize and celebrate existence – present and future – in a loving, excited way. When a space has been changed according to our requirements and we are ready to use it for magick, work, cooking, sleep or whatever else, we have effectively welcomed it as a new presence in our lives.

Think of a blessing as a ritual that confirms to both you and the space that you're ready to settle into it, letting it hold your potential and facilitate your experiences. And you can bless temporary spaces just as much as permanent ones. Bless the hotel room you're staying in for the week, the woodland clearing that you're having a picnic in or the public building your friends are getting married in!

During the blessing you could:

- Ask the beings you work with to bring their strong and positive energy to the space and watch over it.
- Toast the space by raising a glass (which doesn't need to be alcoholic) and making a speech.
- Mark your signature out on the floor of the space with your finger, or visualize it marked there in gleaming light, symbolizing that you are sealing the lovely new energy into the location with your intention.
- Throw a party or have an intimate gathering to celebrate this fresh territory. Inviting friends around for a house/room-warming party can definitely have a magickal quality. I'm not necessarily referring only to human friends! I've certainly invited my goddesses and spirit guides to toast my new place.

WRITE IT

◊ Record an experience of walking into a location and feeling that something wasn't right. What were your thoughts and emotions? How did you behave? In hindsight, what do you think was happening in that situation?

◊ What do you think the world would be like if more people believed that they could energetically own their spaces and change the energy within them?

TRY IT

◊ Probably an obvious one but, yeah, perform a cleansing of your home, a room in your home, or some other space that you occupy. Record your experience and the aftermath. What would you tweak/change for the next time? What would you definitely do again?

◊ If you're out the broom closet, ask someone if you can cleanse their home or one room in their home, and then get feedback from them to see if they noticed any difference, what they appreciated about the energy in the space afterwards, etc. Choose someone who's receptive to this kind of thing, of course.

◊ Start noticing how you can lift 'n' shift the energy in a room just by occupying it and sending your vibes out into it. Sometimes, when an energy feels dull, stagnant or tense, a witch can cut through that yucky stuff just by will alone. This can happen when you're in a room on

> your own or when you're in the middle of a packed event. Witness the effect you can have just by sincerely wanting to feel the energy changing and deciding that this is what is going to happen.

Cleansing Belongings

Although you may regularly feel a particular instinct to cleanse witchcraft tools, such as your wand or Tarot deck, you can actually cleanse anything you own. There are a few reasons that you might want to cleanse an object, witchy or non-witchy:

- You just bought/obtained the object and you'd like to imbibe it with your energy.
- The object was purchased second-hand, so you want to cleanse it of any previous energies.
- Someone borrowed the object and it's just come back into your possession.
- You associate the object with something negative and would like that to change.
- The object has been used over and over again, so its energy feels a bit "gunky" or confused to you.
- You're about to gift the object to someone, so you'd like to set it to a neutral energy and make sure it's ready for its new owner.
- The object broke and had to be repaired, and you feel that a cleansing will form a part of its "healing".
- You lost the object for a long time and feel a little disconnected from it now it's been found, so you feel a cleansing will help to create closeness to it again.
- It's an object that you feel should be cleansed because you want to use it for someone else after using it for yourself, or vice versa (for example, you're about to use your Tarot deck or crystal ball to read for your friend).

MAKE IT HAPPEN

- The object is a hand-me-down or keepsake that used to belong to someone you dislike, or a gift from someone you're not that keen on anymore (I know, it seems mean, but these things happen!).

Helpfully, lots of the ideas for cleansing yourself and your space can be applied or tweaked to help you cleanse belongings. So go back over the suggestions provided in the two segments above. For example, using a cleansing incense or calling on a servitor tasked with cleansing duties are both great for use on objects, too. And here are a few other ideas:

- Write a special statement to be read over an object that needs to be cleansed. Place your hands just above the object, visualizing its energy being cleansed according to your will, while speaking the statement out loud. It doesn't have to be anything fancy – short 'n' sweet is fine. Let's say that you want to cleanse your wand. How about something like, "This wand is bound to me. It holds good vibes only!" If you want something a bit more flowery, you could go for something like, "I claim this wand for my witching art. I call it into my craft and into my heart. It is cleansed for its sacred intention, to carry out spells of my invention. This is my will, let it be so." The words don't need to rhyme – I just happened to be in a bit of a rhyming mood as I was writing that last example. You can also speak to the object directly, calling it "you" to acknowledge its inner spirit, if that feels right. It depends on what you want, really.
- Leave the object on a windowsill or floor in the light of the moon overnight. This is a classic witchy cleansing technique that also fuels the object with intense lunar power, making it a favourite way of cleansing divinatory tools such as decks of cards and sets of runes. But hey, if you want to cleanse your new running shoes in the light of the full moon to make them extra speedy, go for it! There's no rule that says you can only cleanse witchy tools in moonlight. Cleanse kitchen utensils or stationery supplies that way, too, if you want.
- What else might your objects bask under? I've personally left witchy tools cleansing overnight underneath a poster of Freddie Mercury. It just felt right. Amazing results, obviously.

SPIRITUAL HYGIENE

- Wrap the object in a special witchy cleansing cloth or in your favourite item of clothing or blanket, and leave it there overnight so that it soaks up your vibes by the morning.
- Spend the day with the item, keeping it close to you, talking to it or holding it close to your body to establish a sense that it has picked up your energy or been otherwise cleansed of energies that don't align with yours.

You might have a brand-new object that you obtained specifically for use in your craft. Witches often consecrate new witchy tools before adding them to the collection. Consecrating an object means claiming it as a sacred item for spiritual use. For consecration, you can play with any of the ideas given above for cleansing and you might also want to consider these possibilities:

- Hold a tea party for your new arrival! Seriously, sit opposite your new deck, book or wand, pour some tea and just chat to it for a while so that it picks up on your intentions and vibrations, and you feel you've spent some quality time with it. Be open to learning from the object. Does it give you a particular vibe that you'd like to keep? (Certain objects kind of seem to have a personality, don't they? Maybe you want to explore that in each case.)
- Sleep with the object under your pillow for the night. This can create a closeness with it. You wake up in the morning and it feels like the object is more familiar to you and ready to be used.
- Name the object. This can be a good way of giving something your energy, approval and "signature", while also cultivating a sense of closeness with it. Some people name their cars. Well, some witches name their wands! You don't have to overthink the naming process – names don't always need to be deeply symbolic and meaningful. You can totally call your wand Xena or Buffy or Wolverine.
- Do introductions. One way of consecrating a new item would be to talk to it about what its role will be and introduce it to the gang. Let's say you're consecrating your new cauldron. You might say, "I will be mainly using you for fire and water magick, so get ready to be hot and wet! You'll be working closely with my crystals which are going to surround you from now on ..." and then proceed to tell

your cauldron what the crystals mean, what their names are and whatever else information it needs to know. Make the new object feel at home and affirm its role in your craft.

If you want to cleanse whole groups of items together, that's certainly possible. I've many times cleansed my entire altar with everything on it rather than focusing on individual things. I have a protective eye charm that was sent to me by a fellow witch and I like to pass that over the altar while I speak words of power that I devised specifically for cleansing. I sometimes have an incense stick in the other hand, too. I also spray my perfume over the altar sometimes. I don't cleanse my altar space very regularly, as it's in my bedroom which is one of the most high-vibe places in my entire reality. I just don't see the point in piling on the protection when my witchy HQ is also my favourite room in the house – a place where I feel safe, inspired and comfortable. But if I've been away for a while and I feel a sense of disconnection from my altar, a full altar cleanse is something I can pull out the bag. I have a mini-speaker that I pop on there too, so soothing or empowering music is often playing while I pass the eye charm and/or incense over everything and speak the words that bring it all together into energetic harmony again.

WRITE IT

◊ Describe a time when you felt you were holding a blessed or sacred object, whether it was yours or someone else's. Consider why you felt that it was so important. What did the experience of handling the object make you feel?

◊ Describe a time when you felt an object was giving off a negative or dangerous energy or that you didn't want it around you. Were there obvious reasons for this reaction? What actions, if any, did you take? What can you learn from the experience?

TRY IT

◊ Choose an object to cleanse, experimenting with any of the ideas outlined in this book or inventing your own. Don't be afraid to think about what the word "cleanse" means to you. How can you incorporate your personal influences into your cleansing technique for objects? Reach into your emotions around the idea of cleansing something. (Remember that you don't always have to take physical action when cleansing an object; witches can also use visualization to cleanse an object's energy, or mix visualization with physical actions to get the job done.)

◊ Notice what it's like using an object before and after cleansing it. What are the differences?

Creating Sacred Space

When a witch creates sacred space, they're fashioning a protective energetic sphere around themselves so they can work their craft from a place of metaphysical safety. The idea is that an unseen spiritual barrier is set up by marking out the space around yourself, usually in the shape of a circle. The circular form is generally seen to also pass over the witch's head like an invisible dome, shielding them from meddling energies, confusing influences and anything that's superfluous to the working. The circle is visualized as it's made, with energy and intention pouring into its creation. When you cast a circle around yourself, you're then operating in a spiritual sanctuary. Until the circle is closed down, you're "in session". As with everything in this book, however, I encourage you to think about your individual response to the idea of carving out sacred space. Casting a circle may not always feel appropriate – it certainly doesn't for me, and I'll get into the reason for that later in this section. I do cast a circle sometimes, but at other times it's not the right thing. I feel into what is needed.

MAKE IT HAPPEN

Spells and rituals conducted within sacred space are considered less likely to be messed with by outside influences. The notion of an energetic fortress helps a witch to feel secure while doing their work. Sacred space holds only that which is useful for the working and refuses entry to any low vibes and nasty energies that would pull the working off track or distract the witch. The other thing to keep in mind is that witches generate a lot of energy for magickal workings. That energy is believed to be encased inside sacred space, meaning it is concentrated and ready to be directed according to the witch's intentions. Imagine the energy is cream and the witch is a whisk. Creating sacred space is like putting the cream in a small bowl so it's closer to the whisk and gets whipped more quickly and efficiently. Now imagine the cream is in a bathtub – it's much harder to get around it and whip it up with the whisk. (Damn, this is making me want to nom a Victoria sponge.)

How to cast a circle

Here are some super-basic instructions for circle casting (we'll get more elaborate later). Make sure everything you need for your working is with you before casting the circle. Consider having some drinking water in there with you – magickal shenanigans can make even the most experienced witches dehydrated. And it may seem obvious, but visit the bathroom if you need to before you start.

1 Either remaining in the centre of the circle or moving around the perimeter as you cast it, visualize the circle forming clockwise and direct your intention into its creation. If you like, you can point your wand or forefinger to the ground as you go, tracing out where the circle is being constructed.

2 You can say some words if you like. Sometimes I state my intentions for the circle, speaking aloud about what I'm going to do within it, for example: "Tonight, inside this sacred circle, I'm going to weave magick for my future success", or "This circle will house a spell to protect the vulnerable in my community, offering them strength and resources."

3 If you need to leave the circle during your working for any reason, you can cut a door in it with your wand or finger to exit without breaking the structure. You can then seal the door back up in the same way when you re-enter.

4 When you're ready to close the circle, you can go around it anti-clockwise, telling the barrier to disperse.

Despite countless witches acknowledging the power and significance of carving out sacred space, I'm going to head straight for sacrilege, cupcake – it's *not* a prerequisite. It's an option, and there's no doubt that it's been a strongly advised one over the years. But I'm not going to tell you that you absolutely have to make it a part of your practice because I'm more interested in how you feel about the whole thing. As you might have guessed, I'm going to encourage you to lean into your own sense of what's necessary and what empowers you. If you hold the belief that external energies and influences can mess with your magick as you're doing it then it makes sense to form a barrier of sacred space, right? But perhaps you don't always feel like you need it. Maybe sometimes it's necessary and sometimes it's not. Maybe you don't want to be prescriptive about it.

Personally, I don't often create sacred space at my altar before performing spellcraft or ritual anymore. This is because I feel that my entire bedroom is already a potent sacred space that I'm psycho-spiritually maintaining through the time I spend there, the objects I've placed there and the regular witchy and creative activities that occur there. It feels weird for me to carve out a safe, protected space within a safe, protected space. Somehow that just doesn't add up. But when I've done spellcraft in my living room, outside in nature or at someone else's place while I've been staying there, I *did* create sacred space. I felt the protective barrier was necessary and I can confirm that it was helpful. So, I lean into my instinct and go with what I feel is required.

One thing I've learned about sacred space during the many years that I've been witching is that, for me, it does feel so calming and nurturing to be inside it. Although I don't use it for spellcraft at my altar, I do sometimes cast a circle around my bed before going to sleep if I've been having difficult dreams or trouble sleeping. It makes me feel like I'm safe and taken care of, like a baby in the womb somehow. I've also taken to casting sacred space in order to make art or write poetry. I've noticed that my concentration is heightened and I'm in the zone much more if I've cast a circle around myself before I start. So it's not that I rule out the casting of a circle completely. I just like to be clear on my reasons for casting one or not.

If you can cast a circle around yourself with relative ease and feel that the job is done and the sphere is strong, then that's awesome! You can cast a circle whenever you want to perform a magickal working or do anything that requires protection and heightened energy. However, a witch may want to find alternative ways of forming the barrier of energetic safety because casting a circle doesn't quite work for them. Some reasons for this include:

- "I practise in a small room and when I try to visualize a grand energetic circle, I can't help being distracted by the clutter, the walls and the corner of my bed getting in the way!"
- "I have restricted mobility so I can't move around to visualize the circle being formed and that kind of pisses on my Cornflakes a bit."
- "As much as I try to get into the whole 'invisible energetic circle' thing, it doesn't feel real or reliable somehow. I need something I can see."
- "I'm not emotionally attached or attracted to the concept of casting a circle around me so I'm unmotivated to do it."

SPIRITUAL HYGIENE

Here are some alternatives to spark your imagination:

- Select some stones, shells, small toys or other objects, consecrate them and place them in a box or bag. They can then be laid out around you to physically mark a circle or some other shape on the ground. I have some flat grey stones that I collected at a special waterfall in Wales. As I place them down, I whisper to each of them and rub them between my hands, preparing them to do their job of keeping funky energies at bay. If you just want to use string, go ahead with that!
- Visualize your protective energetic circle/bubble forming around you. This can be done without moving at all. The material that forms the barrier can be anything you want. Maybe you'd like bubble wrap or pink cellophane, or you could choose Lego bricks, glittery mist or strong grey hair that weaves around itself ... the possibilities are endless.
- Let the energetic barrier come from within you by connecting to your strong, deep intention to be safe in your workings and then sending that energy outward to surround you.
- Create a servitor who can be summoned to make and hold the sacred space for you when needed. I'm thinking of a little dragon with a long tail who's activated by a song or series of noises, or tempted by some kind of treat! The dragon could dance quickly around you with its tail forming a shimmering circle. Or what about a ghostly figure dressed in a long dark coat?

After you've done your witchy stuff, you can be just as inventive in closing your sacred space as you were in creating it. For me, picking up my waterfall stones and symbolically dusting them off is useful. I thank them for their service and return them to their bag. You could also:

- Literally vacuum or sweep the energetic barrier away (or imagine doing so).
- If your energetic barrier is non-material, do a double clap and shout, "Disperse!" – sweet and simple!

MAKE IT HAPPEN

- Have your sacred-space servitor gobble the energy up, draw it back into them or fly away with it, depending on the characteristics of the being you created for the job.
- Have a specific song that you play to symbolize and instigate the closing of your sacred space. Let the sound of the song melt the sacred-space barrier away for you.

WRITE IT

◊ How important is the creation of sacred space for you at this point on your witchy journey and why?

TRY IT

◊ Choose three different experiments for the creation of sacred space and record your feelings about the results. (If you've been using the same creation method for ages, this might feel challenging, but go for it. Why not change things up?)

TOOLS

Even after being a witch for so many years, I still celebrate the delicious amount of choice available to me when I consider tools for my general practice or for specific workings. I doubt you'll be surprised at this point in the book if I highlight the fact that you don't need *any* tools to have a legitimate practice or to reach maximum strength as a practitioner. Lots of witches only use the power of the mind to direct intention and make things happen. Witchcraft-related objects may not be permitted, desired or obtainable, and that doesn't need to dampen the potency of a practitioner.

Even witches who have a massive collection of tools don't want to be convinced that those tools are a non-negotiable part of making magick. I have lots of witchy stuff, but I believe that I can work magick when I'm not in the presence of any of it. The bells and whistles are nice but not essential, and that's a mindset that I choose to cultivate because I don't want to require physical possessions in order to access my power. I would recommend that witches who haven't tried any tool-free shenanigans do so. You never know when you'll be stuck in a situation where your tools are not within reach and you need to make magick happen pronto.

Now let's take a look at some of the tools available to a witch. This list is nowhere near exhaustive, babycakes! I would certainly recommend that you brainstorm your own ideas and take a look at other lists of tools besides this one.

Tables of correspondences

Most witchy books and websites offer a table of correspondences. This is basically a "who's who" of tools, planets, plants, colours, moon phases and so on, usually separated by category or presented in alphabetical order. A table of correspondences will tell you what the general consensus is around the various elements of the craft. It will tell you what heather can be used for, what rose quartz represents and what each colour is generally believed to mean. There is no table of correspondences in *Rebel Witch* and this is for a good reason. Frankly, in the world of witchcraft you can't swing your broom without hitting one of these tables! They are myriad and many of them offer the same keywords and associations for the same things. (The full moon represents completion, abundance, celebration ... The colour black symbolizes mystery, darkness, death and the spirit realm ... You get the gist.)

These tables can be helpful when you're trying to think of ingredients you might want to place into a spell or you're unsure of the meaning that's commonly assigned to something you might wish to use. However, working too closely with any table could stop you from forging your own relationships with the things you use. Of course, this is the opposite of what the rebel witch outlook is all about. I personally rarely use tables of correspondences anymore but loved reading through them at the beginning of my journey and, at that time, they gave me an idea of consensus opinions in the craft. You can make your own decision about how often you use these tables and lists. Many witches like to make their own table as they go along, recording the perceptions they gained through first-hand experiences rather than just following what others have said.

Symbols

There are tons of symbols that witches have been using in their practice for donkey's years. Magickal symbols are high-powered indeed. I have the alchemical symbols for salt and fire tattooed onto my fingers, as they have great significance to me. I also regularly use runes in my practice, carving them into candles that I use for magick and devotion, tracing them over objects that I am consecrating, or visualizing their shapes going across the floor when I'm forging a barrier of protection around a room. You can find amazing lists of symbols and their meanings online. As a rebel witch myself, I do find that designing my own symbols for specific purposes can be even more effective than using pre-existing ones. However, if I'm having an uninspired day and can't think of a symbol to draw, I'll revert back to one I've used successfully before or go for the old faithful – my signature (works like a charm).

Broom

The classic and unmistakable piece of witchy gear. The usual name for a witch's broom is a besom and both the name and distinctive shape (twigs tied to a stick) differentiate it from an ordinary modern household broom, although of course you can feel free to use that too. You can also use a dustpan brush, a large flat paint brush or any kind of soft hairbrush. Brooms can be used to sweep away yucky energies, clear the room for creating sacred space and whatnot. If you have a small travel altar or temporary altar space, you can use a little make-up brush as a mini-besom. I know, so cute, right?

Wand

Wands help you to direct your energy and intention. You can point a wand at the floor to carve sacred space or to ground your energy after a magickal working. Point it to the sky to represent "going up in the world", raising your vibration or pointing to your highest intentions. Using your wand, you can also draw energetic lines of demarcation between one place and another, or between one state of being and another. Visualize a powerful light flowing from the tip of your wand as you use it, if you like. You can give your wand a name and wrap it in a special cloth or box for safekeeping, or have it out on your altar at all times. A stick you find on a walk in the forest can be your wand – simply consecrate it if you feel called to, and it's ready to be used. If you want to make it more fancy, you can varnish or paint it, wrap the handle area with material, or glue crystals onto it. Or you can shell out for a fancy wand made by a witchy artisan, just use a chopstick or grab a plastic wand from a dress-up shop.

String/thread

If something needs to be unified or healed, string can be used to represent the bonding force/energy. (I once felt like I didn't belong in my home anymore, so I used a Tarot card to represent the home and a card to represent me and my feelings. I bound the two cards with string to represent my desire to feel bonded to the environment again. The bound cards were left under the light of the full moon for a night and then under my pillow for a second night. This spell was very effective.) String is also used for bindings (see page 214), for designating sacred space and for marking out other things on the floor, such as areas of "past", "present" and "future" in your rune or card readings. String can represent healing energy – place it around something that requires healing or gestation. You might want to use it to thread pendants or beads for necklaces that you can then wear during rituals. String can also be used to tie flowers or herbs together, to then gift to someone in your life or to a deity as an offering. So many uses!

Blades

There are plenty of practical reasons for keeping a sharp blade and/or pair of scissors in your toolkit; you'll need it if you're preparing herbs or flowers for an offering or spell, for example, or if something needs to be cut *during* a spell. (I often work with a ball of string in spellcraft, so it's common for me to take scissors into sacred space.) You can also use a ceremonial blade – an athame – which is intended for *metaphorical* rather than literal cutting, and is therefore not usually sharp. My athame is a beautiful antique letter-opener and I use it to represent division/ separation and my power to end something or to carve out a wall of protection around myself, someone else or a project/situation. I also like to use my athame to direct magickal energy in the same way as a wand is used (I actually don't own a wand as this tool doesn't resonate with me – I find knives to be much more powerful objects).

Candles

As an aesthetic choice, candles are often the light source of preference for witches in rituals, spellcraft, devotionals, etc. It's rare to meet a magick-maker who doesn't happen to love the way candlelight dances around and the vibe that a candlelit environment offers. But candles can also be tools in spellcraft. You can assign certain meanings to different colours of candle and then perform candle magick (which we will explore on pages 158–9). Candles can represent the light of realization, the heat of protection or the emergence of hope. They can symbolize timelines, intentions, people and life journeys. I can't wait for us to get into this in more depth later!

Potions

Although people often think of a potion as a concoction of various different liquids, it can actually be just *one* liquid. You may want to combine different herbs, fruit juices and other ingredients into potions that you create for spells, but you can certainly keep it simple too. In fact, any liquid or ointment could count as a potion without you having to put much time into making it – frankly, you could crack a cream soda and just do some witchy stuff on it. Obviously, if you're going to ingest your potion or rub it onto the skin, make sure you research all the ingredients to make sure that they're safe. Potions can also be placed into bath water, poured onto the ground (provided they're not bad for the soil), sprinkled onto clothing or around a room, or used as massage oil, depending upon the ingredients and texture.

My favourite base for a potion is carrier oil. I may add perfumes and essential oils to it and then rub it into my hair or onto my pulse points. I make bottles containing customized oils for friends and partners, selecting ingredients that speak to their specific needs and then putting a powerful blessing into the bottle before delivering it with instructions on how to use it. I also like to make potions from moon water, which is simply water that has been left out overnight in the light of the full moon so that it's infused with those lush lunar vibes. Snow water and storm water are great bases for potions too – simply collect snow in a container and let it melt, or leave a container out during a storm. I'll leave you to decide what such waters would be used for in your practice, as I think it's all down to interpretation. But for me personally, moon water is kind of an all-purpose potion base, snow water is for cleansing and purification, and storm water is something I use to encourage greater power and – sometimes – to bring about a sudden end to something, usually for my own protection or for the protection of others. Don't forget that you can also make solid food into a magickal substance by investing it with magickal intention and then consuming it or giving it to others to consume.

Bottles, jars, boxes, bags and other containers

There's no smoke without fire when it comes to the stereotype that witches love to collect pretty bottles and jars. I personally have a few more than I need – and I'm not sorry. When the time comes for something to be contained in your practice, you'll be glad you've saved a jar or bottle that used to hold something in your kitchen. I also like to collect vintage cut-glass perfume bottles, which are great for containing enchanted perfumes and potions. Any bottle with a pipette is a good one for the collection because you can use the dropper to place liquid with precision, for example when applying it to a poppet during a spell. Bags and boxes are also useful, not just for storage but also as tools for spells. Containers can be used for shielding, strengthening, purifying or hiding whatever is inside. I personally have a box with a skull-head on it that I use for cooling things off and making them less intense. If I have a recurring thought that's distracting me, I write it on a piece of paper and put it in the skull-head box for a few days with a selection of relevant crystals on top. Another decorative box is my "charging box", which I've invested with positive intentions and strength. I place items of jewellery into it, for myself and others, so they soak up the energy from the box.

Cauldron

The classic image of a large, onion-shaped black cauldron with bubbling florescent liquid and filmy smoke oozing from it is, let's face it, totally awesome! It does fill my witchy heart with a cackle of joy. But you may want to opt for a mini version if you fancy the quintessential three-legged cauldron style, to save space and be able to store it away when you're not using it. They're fireproof and tend to be wonderfully hard-wearing, plus you can find some lovely designs with pentacles on them and whatnot. Any fireproof, hardy bowl is appropriate to use for cauldron-y stuff though – it doesn't have to be the typical black iron design. Some of the key things you could use a cauldron for include:

- Storing and charging ingredients that you're collecting and prepping for a spell working, in much the same way as I described using boxes and other containers as magickal charging devices above.
- Burning lists of the things you want to get rid of. Write the list on a piece of paper, pop a charcoal disc into the cauldron, light the disc and then put in the paper. (Make sure the cauldron is placed on a fireproof surface away from flammable objects, so that any pesky escaping embers don't land on your altar cloth!)
- Formulating your potions. Yes, that's right, this is the classic use for a cauldron – as a magickal mixing bowl! You can also leave the potion in there for a while, maybe in the light of the moon, to set or charge the potion before you bottle it.
- As a handy incense holder. (Bit basic, but yeah.) I have a certain incense that's consecrated for the purpose of covering me in protection when I'm about to enter a tense or unpredictable situation. With that incense in particular, it feels way more significant to walk through it when it's being burned in my cauldron rather than in another holder.
- As a good mortar for grinding up herbs, petals, etc. Grab your pestle or some other object that can be used to crush and grind things, and away you go. If you're the type of rebel witch to put magickal vibes into your meals, then you may want to prepare

the herbs and spices or dressings for your food inside the cauldron rather than in an ordinary kitchen dish. If so, maybe you'd want your cauldron to live in the kitchen.

Learning resources

Books, websites, videos, podcasts, online chat groups, meet-up groups, workshops and courses are all possible resources to help you deepen your understanding and witch with gusto. (I love using "witch" as a verb!) You get to choose your weapons here. If you find that learning from books can be taxing, maybe podcasts or videos about your subjects of interest would help more. If you learn best through conversations, then joining a group (online or offline) or hiring a witchy teacher/mentor could be useful avenues to consider. You can mix and match your resources. Don't be afraid to learn critically, comparing resources and examining discrepancies. Know that you can learn about the consensus on something without having to hold yourself to it if it simply doesn't feel right for you.

If you're not a big one for tons of reading and research, that's OK. You don't have to be a major bookworm or a perpetual student to be an effective witch. Plenty of witches have done the damn thing without cracking open a single book on the topic in their lives. Some were taught by a relative or friend, and some just do what they instinctively feel moved to do, and it works. There are witches out there who don't feel the need to seek a second opinion or know what other witches are doing, while others want to talk about the craft daily and get lots of perspectives. No one is wrong here. It's down to who you are and what you're looking for.

Clothes, jewellery and accessories

Don't forget that you can dress for how you want to feel when doing your witchy thing. Some witches like to work their magick with no clothes on at all, which is often known as practising "skyclad". I'm the type that prefers to dress in a distinctly powerful and ritualistic kind of way, which involves accessorizing and putting colours together. Over the years, I've collected lots of pieces of power jewellery and loud clothing. Many of these items were selected to make me feel potent for my rituals and workings, and have found their way into my sacred space. You might want a specific piece of clothing, jewellery or some other accessory that you can wear whenever you're doing magick – something that symbolizes that you're in the zone. Or you can change it up and wear something different each time, depending on mood and intention. You can also enchant clothing that can be worn later in a specific scenario or around a certain person in order to achieve a desired result. For instance, maybe you want to put a dash of romantic energy into the seams of the outfit you're wearing on a first date, or make sure your team kit for the big game is filled with strong victory vibes.

Kids toys, ornaments, bric-a-brac

If you need a trinket to represent something in a spell/ritual or to place on your altar as a tool, you can use objects that come from your past and family experiences, such as keepsakes, birthday gifts and souvenirs, or you can go out shopping. You can choose to buy new objects if you want to, but I think there's great power in pre-owned things. If you find that some objects seem to possess an energy that you can tap into, then the process of hunting for second-hand objects to be used in a magickal process might be highly interesting to you. Psychometry is the process of reading the energetic experience of an object: its memories, which offer information on who owned it previously and what kind of environment it belonged to. If you find something you're into, you could try holding the object or being close to it, closing your eyes and simply asking it where it has been and what it might have to teach you. You may see flashes of the object's former owner or feel strong emotions as you lean in to the object's energy. You may not get a strong reading of the object's energy at all, and that's OK. Buy it anyway if you have the coins and you like it!

Poppets

A poppet is a kind of doll that's used for magickal and ritual purposes. Witches often make their own poppets from cloth, stuffing the body to fill out the shape. You can also purchase poppets from other makers or simply use dolls that you find in charity shops or from your childhood if you've held on to anything from that time. But a poppet doesn't have to have a human shape at all. I once found a heart-shaped pin cushion while thrifting and felt it was perfect for some healing magick I was doing for myself following a tough heartbreak. I washed the pin cushion, sprayed it with my perfume and wrote my initials on it to seal the witchy deal. I worked with that thing for ages, pinning uplifting words onto it, scattering lavender over it and even singing to it! Needless to say, my heartbreak faded, and now I keep the pin cushion in my altar drawer for whenever I'm feeling emotionally fragile and need a lift. I also use a poppet shaped like the human body, often focusing on the lower back area because I have a back injury that sometimes flares up and magick is a key part of my pain-management routine.

How to make a basic poppet

I work with two poppets that both symbolize me and both contain my blood, hair and nails. If your poppet is going to be reused in different workings and be representative of different people, then it obviously makes less sense to include someone's hair etc in the stuffing, but it's a great idea if you do want the poppet to symbolize someone specific.

1 Grab a clean, ironed pillowcase and draw out the shape you want the poppet to be. Make sure it's big enough for your magickal workings – remember that it needs to be filled with stuffing.

2 Once the shape is drawn, cut along the outline, making sure you cut through both sides of the pillowcase so you're left with two identically shaped pieces of cloth.

3 Pop some pins around the outline, connecting the two cloth pieces together, back to back.

4 Once you've pinned the two pieces together, you're ready to connect them permanently. You can hand sew them, or use a sewing machine or even a stapler. Make sure you leave a hole big enough for the stuffing to go in!

5 Pull the cloth through the stuffing hole that you left open, turning the poppet inside out so you can't see the stitching/staples and pen marks. (This is optional. If you fancy something a bit more rough 'n' ready, or the chosen shape of your poppet is hard to turn inside out, don't worry about it!)

6 Now for the stuffing. I tend to go for corn or some other dry grain. Shredded waste paper can be a useful stuffing material, too. I've also been known to use cotton wool, but I don't buy that anymore because it's not environmentally friendly. You can put herbs, little crystals, folded-up notes etc into the stuffing, as well as the hair or fingernails of whoever the poppet represents.

7 Once the poppet is adequately stuffed, sew/staple the hole and there you have it – you're all set with your very own poppet!

Flowers, fruits, herbs, spices, etc

You can make spell mixes using these kinds of ingredients, to then be burned in your cauldron as incense, scattered over/around something during a ritual/spell, made into teabags or placed into food (depending on how edible the ingredients are). You could grow flowers, herbs and so yourself, investing the plants with your witchy intentions, and then giving them as gifts to others or ingesting them to receive the energies you placed into them as they grew. You'll also find that witches who are

MAKE IT HAPPEN

more green-fingered than you are likely selling what you need, if you're lacking the space or inclination to grow stuff yourself. The common meanings for each flower or herb can be found by searching online or checking tables of correspondences, but don't forget to factor in your own views on each of them. What do they symbolize to you? What do they usually help you with? What do they remind you of? What do you like about them?

It's also wise to take a look at the ecological and cultural implications of seeking out something that you want to work with. Palo santo, palo de rosa and boswellia (from which frankincense is made) are among the list of endangered species that witches have been purchasing. Many witches are dialoguing much more these days about our impact on others and on the planet when we choose to pursue ingredients that are endangered, over-harvested or sacred to marginalized spiritual groups. It's great to ensure you've fully researched this.

Crystals, shells, bones and stones, etc

Use these natural objects in your spells and rituals, if you like. Finding special natural items like these on your travels can be so exciting! I have a perfectly round, flat grey stone that truly looks as though it was carved into a circular shape, but was just fashioned that way by nature. It's now my "shuffling stone" – I place my Tarot cards on it when I'm dovetail shuffling them. As I live very near the sea, collecting shells is also a big one for me. There are shells all over my altars in my home and I give them as presents and make them into sacred jewellery, too. Some of the stones I own are representative of intentions and moods, and I use them to symbolize those things in spells. Try using a heavy stone to represent discipline and determination, for example. Place the stone on top of a folded list of all the tasks you have to do, to symbolize their successful completion.

In the past, I've purchased crystals and I do use them in my practice. However, now I know much more about the problems with unethical and unsustainable crystal mining, I prefer to just work with my existing collection and what I actually find myself in nature, rather than buying any new crystals. If I needed something crystal-wise and couldn't find it in my own collection, I would check out the second-hand market.

Hair, nails, tears, saliva, blood and – ahem – other bodily fluids

Anything containing a person's DNA can offer a highly effective tool for performing all kinds of magick, from banishing and binding to healing and love spells. Mixing two or more people's blood together can be considered a strong symbol of bonding, commitment, joint power and unbreakable oaths. You can use strands of hair to tie something together in a spell or to thread through clothing. Hair and nails can be placed into a spell bag containing herbs, petals, etc, which can then be placed under someone's pillow or hung up on a hook. I once made a spell bag for someone who was missing me a lot while I was away from them. It contained a strengthening blend of dried herbs, fruits and petals, and also included my hair and nails, as well as a handwritten note that "programmed" the bag's contents to help the individual through the time of separation. (I know, I am just irresistible.) Obviously, it's important to always consider safety when working with blood, semen, etc. Don't ingest anything you're unsure of and use gloves if necessary. I know we're rebel witches, but there are some rules it's best to keep.

Soil, grass, sand, etc

The earth of a place that's special or significant to you in some way can make a great spell ingredient or protective/strengthening substance to keep in your home somewhere. I used to have the sand of several important beaches in little bottle pendants that I wore as a kind of pick-me-up when I was feeling sad. I've also taken sand from the beach where I live now and put it into my cauldron to stand incense sticks up in. You could take soil from your garden if you're moving house and you'd like to keep something that feels like it's full of the energy of the old place. Many witches also take earth from the graves of loved ones. Graveyard earth in general can be powerful, but witches tend to agree that it's not clever to take it directly from the graves of people you didn't know, even if only because it's disrespectful.

Journals, notebooks, online documents and other recordkeeping methods

There's a whole section dedicated to recordkeeping (see Chapter 16), so there we'll do the deep dive into all the options and what's currently working for you, what needs to change and why. For now, let me just say that recordkeeping - in written, audio or digital format - is not essential, but it's highly popular in witchcraft for a reason. The reality is that it's super useful to read back over what you've tried and what the results were. The very act of recording is also a good way of realizing certain things about what happened. We shouldn't feel pressure to keep a record of everything and some witches are more fastidious about it than others.

Sacred texts

The Bible is a sacred text for Christians, the Quran for Muslims and the Torah for Jews. What would *your* sacred text be, as a rebel witch? If there's a particular book that really inspires, empowers and enchants you, don't be afraid to decide that it's a sacred part of your practice - and of course, there's no need to limit yourself to just one. For me, the *Chronicles of Narnia* are absolutely magickal and sacred. I've studied them in great depth. I've inscribed passages from them into my grimoires and incorporated quotes into prayers, spells and mantras. Aslan is a character of rich significance to me as a witch. I've journeyed with him in my dreams and during my spiritual journeys, and called on him for energy and guidance when I've been feeling scared or unsure. I also consider *Alice's Adventures in Wonderland* to be a sacred text in my practice. Again, I've studied the story and considered its symbolism. I've worked with Alice as a guide when going on spiritual journeys to find answers - and yes, I've been to tea with the Mad Hatter and the March Hare! I also use Dylan Thomas's complete poems and a book of artists' manifestos. These also work really well as sacred texts.

You don't have to choose a work of long fiction to be your sacred text. You could also consider:

- Books of poetry, quotes or lyrics
- Short stories, plays or essays
- Biographies and diaries of famous people you admire
- Picture books
- Comic books and graphic novels
- Encyclopaedias

You may find that your choice of sacred text changes over time. You might study a text to the bone, embrace it as a daily part of your practice, and then finally reach the sense that you've extracted what was required from it, grandfathering it into your collection of witchy resources but ultimately lessening your dedication to it and taking on a different text to start the process all over again. You can always return to sacred texts that you haven't used in a while if you feel called to them.

How to choose a sacred text and what to do with it

If the idea of choosing a sacred text appeals to you, but you're unsure of what kind of text would be good, here's a few considerations:

◊ You could choose a book that you feel deep affection for and know quite well but would like to explore in more depth.

◊ Alternatively, you might want to pick a book in a seemingly random way, in the belief that you'll be divinely guided to the one that you should use.

MAKE IT HAPPEN

◊ Think about which books have particularly inspiring, empowering and magickal qualities for you.

◊ Bear in mind that you can absolutely have a probation period for a sacred text to see if it works for you. There's no need to pressure yourself to get this choice right first time. Just because you love a particular book doesn't mean it will be a good witchy tool, so maybe give yourself a few weeks to see how it's going before deciding if you'll continue with it or move on to something else.

Once you've chosen your text, what happens next? Obviously, that's entirely up to you, cupcake. You might want to consider any of the following options:

◊ Have regular study sessions, going through the book and delving into your perceptions about it. Make notes about what each part is teaching you.

◊ Read the book aloud during rituals or spells, using certain parts of the text as incantations or powerful speeches.

◊ Read it before bed, in coffee shops, on your commute – take it everywhere with you.

◊ Read any reviews or essays that you can find about your sacred text, online or in books or journals. Do you agree with other people's views on it? What might you add to what others have written?

◊ See if you can challenge yourself to memorize passages or sentences, and give them special meaning so that you can recite them when needed.

◊ Write regularly about your journey with your sacred text, figuring out what it's teaching you, why it's important and where you are with the process of connecting to it.

◊ Use the text to answer questions, solve problems or receive guidance. This is also known as bibliomancy (see page 193).

You might want to avoid working with a copy of the book that's precious to you. Perhaps you'll want to highlight key passages in the book, put notes in the margin or use sticky notes and tabs, and at the very least, you'll be picking it up a lot, so you can expect it to get dog-eared. Several friends have gifted me delicious hardback editions of *Alice's Adventures in Wonderland* over the years, knowing how much I love the book. But when I'm working with the text, I use a battered paperback copy that's intended for spiritual practice.

Books, films, TV shows, art, music, etc

Your whole rebel witch practice can be absolutely steeped in the things you love and find most interesting. Thread the stuff that inspires and empowers you through the tapestry of your orthopraxy. In addition to any chosen sacred texts, you might have a plethora of other influential books on your list of magickal tools. Dip in and out of them. Use passages from them as the basis for spells or rituals. Transport yourself to the worlds within them, using the locations and scenarios as places of power in your practice – where you have experiences, learn lessons and take actions in the world of your imagination. What really sets your soul alight? Think of albums, novels, clothes from certain eras, characters from TV shows ... What kinds of themes and vibes make you feel empowered? Otherworldly? Enchanted? Beautiful? Excited? Visuals can be really powerful here – you might choose a particular piece of art to go on your altar because it helps you to embody your witchhood in some way. There could be totally obscure reasons why something deeply resonates with you, and the great thing is that you don't owe anyone an explanation for that. You are the world-builder – and the world is absolutely yours.

Divinatory tools

There's an entire chapter on divination (see Chapter 15), so we can really get into it then. But for now, I'll just say that divinatory tools are used to look into the future, figure out the probabilities of certain scenarios and learn the best strategies for success. They include Tarot and oracle cards, crystal balls, pendulums and runes. As a witch, you can also absolutely practise divination *without* any of these things and we'll also take a look at a few ways of doing that.

Mirror

I've included this because it's something I work with so much in my own practice that it would feel strange not to. Having said that, I also work with disco balls and nun dolls – I'm certainly not planning to include *all* the weird 'n' wondrous aspects of my practice in this book as it might be a much thicker volume than anyone would want to read! But the mirror is something that might strike you as more broadly useful. You can gaze into a mirror in order to do deep work on yourself. Speaking encouraging and loving words to your own reflection can be a powerful way to strengthen in the face of challenges. Of course, it doesn't need to be a physical mirror. Plenty of people close their eyes and visualize themselves in order to send loving words and vibes to their own energy, and that's also a great way of doing it. I personally find that looking into my own eyes is a potent way to feed myself truth and toughness when I feel like I'm in the middle of a total shit storm.

Mirrors can also be used to scry. One way that I don't think I'll ever try is to turn the lights off, sit in candlelight, and gaze at the darkness behind your reflection to see what's there. Err ... nope. Maybe this sounds odd coming from a witch, but I'm afraid of the dark and I think my overactive imagination would simply combine all the scariest things I've seen in horror movies and put them together behind me! But if you want to try it, be my guest.

Ouija board

If you're interested in making contact with the dead, this tool is a classic. It's one of those objects that's as controversial as it is popular. You probably know at least one person who used a shop-bought or homemade board with their friends growing up, usually to contact a deceased grandparent or just ask if there was *anyone* willing to come forward "from the other side" with a message. A Ouija board can be used to give an apparently disgruntled ghost an opportunity to speak their piece. Let's say you move into a new property and quickly realize that doors slam by themselves, objects seem to move around in the night, or you just feel a lingering presence there. You might use a Ouija board to ask what's up and see if you get an answer. The idea is that a ghost will only make their presence known if they have something they need to say, after which they'll vacate in peace. But some warn against the use of Ouija boards to contact energies you're unfamiliar with, there being a possibility that you'll contact something that never was human and certainly doesn't have friendly intentions.

Mind-altering substances

While not being in any way a prerequisite, alcohol, cannabis and psychedelics such as mushrooms and LSD, among other things, are used by many witches to reach altered states of consciousness during rituals, spiritual journeying, deep meditations and other situations. Psychedelics, in particular, have a long history of being used as modes of transportation to a higher/altered state in order to receive answers.

The power and value of such substances in spiritual work has been both overstated and understated – both glorified and demonized. On the one hand, those who have an interest in ingesting something to heighten their spiritual connection may tell themselves that it's needed in order to receive a really profound experience. They may be at risk of feeling as though nothing is as good or useful when they're not under the influence. On the other hand, the naysayers are often stuck on the idea that any witch who ingests anything in the interests of spiritual experience has gone badly off-kilter and needs to recognize that no substance is ever necessary at any time. These extremes of opinion don't seem necessary to me. It's clear that seeing a substance as sacramental and using it as part of witchcraft has a spectrum of pros and cons, and will be down to individual perspective.

Some substances are obviously illegal and, for many people, that's a major consideration. Also, if you're interested in pursuing a substance-induced altered state, it's worth thinking about your experience with it outside the ritual/sacred setting. Acquainting yourself with a mind-altering substance for the first time while performing a ritual or journeying to the astral can be pretty high-impact and not necessarily always advisable. Your mental health and emotional wellbeing are important factors, too. If you know you're dealing with ongoing issues and tend to struggle with your thoughts and feelings, the decision to try anything that alters your state is a serious one.

Do all the necessary research about anything you're interested in. Researching something doesn't mean you've made the decision to try it. It means you want to be informed, and that can only be a good thing. Here are some possible avenues of research that might be important:

- What's the origin and history of this substance?
- What are the laws regulating it where I live?
- What studies have been done on this substance?
- Do people run workshops or give talks on this substance?
- What's the environmental impact of harvesting/producing the substance?
- What kinds of experiences do people describe when under its influence?

You could also ask yourself these questions:

TOOLS

- What do I already know about this substance?
- What do I still need to find out about it?
- What are my previous experiences with this substance, if any?
- Why am I considering adding this substance to my practice as a tool?
- What could go right?
- What could go wrong?
- Do I need to open up a dialogue with others about my decision-making process?
- How can I ensure that any use of substances in my practice would be measured and healthy?
- How will I know if my relationship with a substance – either spiritually or generally – has veered into unhealthy territory?

WRITE IT

◊ Imagine you had to choose just one tool to use for six months of witchy practice. You can only use that one and no others. Which one do you choose and why?

◊ Examine how much you currently rely on tools in your practice. Is your relationship with your tools healthy and positive? Or is it too much?

◊ How confident are you that you could practise without any tools? Explain your answer.

◊ Write a letter to one of your favourite witchy tools. Tell it why you appreciate it and why it's an important part of your practice.

TRY IT

◊ Decide to use a tool you've never used before. Set a time
for the trial period and choose one to three things you'll
do with the tool to try it out. At the end of the trial,
decide how well it worked. What did you get from the
experience? Will you keep using the tool?

◊ Decide to take a well-used tool out of your practice for
a set time and see how you do without it! What did you
learn from this experience?

12

ALTARS

I don't think I'm making much of a wild guess when I suspect that *Rebel Witch*'s readers will consider this one of the most exciting parts of the whole book. Magpies are legion among witches – we like shiny things. We especially like to gather shiny things together and arrange them in satisfying collections to behold, admire and work with. Altars can be impressive, inspiring and deeply moving. In this section, we're going to explore altars in all their weird glory, and I literally can't wait. But here's where I need to give a few disclaimers.

Firstly, you're not obliged to be attracted to the notion of having an altar or even using tools whatsoever in your craft. You're no less of a practitioner if you don't care for witchy objects. In fact, it's obviously advantageous to be a witch who doesn't rely on physical stuff to make magick happen, as the magick may be needed when the stuff isn't to hand. Clinging too tightly to the bits and bobs can start to convince you that they're essential and that without them, you're not a witch at all. You might want to cultivate that mindset for a *specific* working, as it can be powerful to put a lot of meaning into an object while using it. But feeling that way about objects all the time isn't too tasty. What if you need to do a protection spell on public transport, a calming visualization while lying in a hospital bed or a release ritual while away on holiday? At such times, the power of your intention is what matters. Craving your witchy stuff will just interrupt your potency.

Secondly, if you can't have a physical altar due to restrictions on space, money, mobility or privacy, this says precisely nothing about your witchy potential or ability. Nothing at all. (Seriously, nothing.) Witches have to live in all kinds of different realities and some of them simply can't include an altar. Maybe you know that having one would mean you'd face questioning or reprisals from someone close to you who's hostile toward witchcraft. Maybe you feel you wouldn't have time to tend to an altar and it would end up covered in dust, taking up unnecessary room. Maybe you're strapped for the spare space or cash to make an altar into a reality right now. Perhaps you just haven't figured out if you really want/need one or what would be placed onto it. All these reasons are fine. Any reasons are fine.

You might wonder why I'm stressing this point. Well, to be honest, stressing the point is just a part of my personality and as you've read this far, you'll have probably realized that! But this point about not needing an altar is particularly important to highlight because the material shit can end up being the focus in witchcraft. It can get in the way. Witches end up feeling intimidated or inadequate if they don't have the shinies and pretties, if they don't have a place to go each day in their home to recognize their witchhood, and so on. I really want you to know that you're a witch with or without an altar, OK? If you want to skip the rest of this section because it doesn't apply to you, please do that. *Definitely* consider doing that if you really want an altar and can't have one right now – I don't want you to get "altar FOMO" (I've had that in the past and it sucks!). But I just want to let you know that toward the end of this section, you'll find information about temporary, hidden, travel and astral altars – providing possible alternatives that might flick your witchy switch.

Why have an altar at all? There are many reasons that witches work with altars, and some of the reasons overlap. The reasons also change over time. Here are just a few:

- As a reminder to practise regularly (seriously, an altar can call you to it).

ALTARS

- As a potent place for workings, devotionals, etc, charged and shielded with magick.
- As one convenient place for all the witchy tools and thingamajigs to live.
- As your sacred witchy space that others know should be respected and not touched (it may be obvious, but pets and young children won't get this memo, so try to put the altar somewhere they won't get to it).
- As a spiritual home and a comforting place to go when the world is crappy.
- As an external representation of your inner witchy life, symbolizing the shape that your practice is taking, your belief structure, your deities, etc.
- As an opportunity to be creative – experimenting with the visual aesthetics, making things to be placed on there, etc.
- As an awesome reflection space to sit while crying, journaling, sipping your morning tea and trying to figure out your shit.
- As a way of claiming and owning your identity as a witch, helping you to feel more comfortable with being on the path, feeling proud of who you are.
- As a way of honouring the beings you work with, using images of the beings and offerings to them to create a shrine-like vibe that celebrates them.

If you have an altar at the moment, you can still use the reflections in this section to help you check in with your views on the practice of keeping and using it. Even if you've used an altar for decades, it's great to consider any necessary changes you might want to make to the space itself or your mindset around it. So, let me go on an altar ramble. Take from it what you will, dollface.

Altar Purpose, Aesthetics and Type

Altars are usually set up on the top of a table, shelf or chest of drawers, but some witches make their altars on the floor, rather than having them elevated. You can sit at your altar in a chair or wheelchair, or you can sit on the floor. Or you may wish to stand at it. It all depends on where it's positioned, how you want to feel and what works for you.

You don't necessarily have to carry out any actions on the altar itself. Some witches do and some don't. In my case, most of the things on my altar pretty much remain in the same position – such as the large mirror I have in the centre at the back, the statuettes of my main working deities at the sides and other objects that symbolize different parts of my belief structure and practice. I only have a small working space at the front that's marked out by a glass plate. On the plate, I do Tarot and oracle readings, and sometimes I pop my cauldron on there to do workings with it using fire and water. I also use the glass plate to bless and charge objects for myself or other people.

But most of the things that I do with objects at my altar are done on the floor in front of it, rather than on top of it. This is simply because there's more space and it feels right for me to spread things out on the floor rather than feel cramped on the altar itself. However, you might choose to use your entire altar for workings and have things moving around all the time.

Some witchy spaces could be more accurately described as shrines, because they're places of reverence dedicated to specific figures/ beings. At shrines, you can give offerings and spend time forging a deeper connection to the being honoured by the space, talking to them or meditating on their energy. In my hallway, for instance, I have a shrine to Freddie Mercury. For me, he epitomizes creative energy and empowered glamour. You can dedicate a shrine to an ancestor, a public figure or even a fictional character. A shrine may not just be for one person but for an entire group of people, such as the whole cast of a film or the entire ancestral line on one side of your family. A shrine can also be dedicated to an era in history, or a concept within art or design – you get the picture. Let your imagination go off road. Shrines can also be built into a larger altar, of course.

You don't actually have to be near any of your altar spaces at all when doing rituals, spells, devotionals, etc – you can choose to do them in a completely different space in your home and just keep the altar for reflection. That's pretty rare, of course. Most witches with an altar want to be there when they perform workings in their homes. But I want to keep gently reminding you that this is *your* show and you can run it exactly as you like. You may want to have multiple altars if you have the space and desire for that!

The aesthetics of your altar are totally down to you. If you're not fussed about what the altar looks like and instead want to focus solely on the practical considerations of what needs to be on it and how it will be used, that's fine. There's no pressure to be concerned about its visual appearance. But it might be worth noting that the feeling you get when you approach your altar can be influenced by the way it looks, so pay attention to what different colours, themes and references do to your state of mind and general mood. You may find that a specific colour, pattern or style seems generally more inspiring or empowering. You can choose to stick with something for as long as it has that beneficial effect. But you can change up the aesthetics very regularly if you like, and many witches do. They switch out the altar cloth they've been using, rearrange their tools or redecorate with different pieces of art, things found while on nature walks or objects from second-hand stores. Altars obviously do gather dust, so changing the objects or their placement is also a good time to clean the space. I do know a few witches who avoid the use of an altar cloth so they can stick down the objects using tack and then run a feather duster over and between things easily without any breakages! (Just a tip for you if you hate fiddly cleaning tasks ...)

Here are some things to consider when figuring out an altar space:

- What inspires you most about having an altar?
- How could your witchy journey be enhanced by having an altar?
- What do you like about the altar spaces you've seen?
- What do you definitely want to *avoid* when designing/ maintaining an altar space?
- What's the space you have available for an altar and how can you maximize it?

MAKE IT HAPPEN

- Will there be space for working on top of it or in front of it?
- How can you be physically comfortable if you're at the altar for long periods of time?
- Is it out of the reach of animals and children?
- What do you already have in your possession for the base of the altar and for tools/props to go in and on it, etc?
- How do you want to feel when you see and use it?
- What would you like it to say to you and, if applicable, to others?
- Are you going for a sparse/minimalist look or something a bit more ornate?
- Which key words would you use to describe your desired altar aesthetic?
- How often might you want to change the placement of objects and/or aesthetic?
- Should all objects, colours etc on your altar be connected?
- Do you feel that everything on your altar should have deep meaning? Or can some things just look nice?

How to set up your altar

1 First of all, consider if you'd like any of these things on the altar:

- Altar cloth
- Fairy lights
- Candles
- Photos, pieces of art and statuettes
- Found objects from nature, such as stones, shells and bones
- Any of the tools you intend to use regularly

2 Consider which items you'd like to have nearby but out of sight. Not everything needs to be directly on the altar space. You can keep items in a storage container under your bed, or in drawers or otherwise out the way until needed.

3 Draw the shape of the altar on a piece of paper and start brainstorming by arranging the space into sections where specific themes will be symbolized or certain objects will live. If you don't feel like making a drawing, just start playing with the objects and see how you feel when trying to find the right arrangement. Take photos of your design decisions along the way, so you can go back and see how the set-up looked at various stages.

4 Once everything is the way you think you want it, try some practical actions to see if the set-up is useful. For instance, if you have candles, can you reach your arm out to light them without knocking things over? Can you access your regular tools easily? Can you see the stuff that needs to be visible to you while you're sitting in front of the space?

5 Then, sit with the set-up and lean into your feelings. How does it make you feel? Are there any tweaks that need to be made?

Temporary altars

Not all altars are permanent. You can set up temporary ones that are intended to serve a specific purpose before being dismantled again. For instance, you may want an altar for a 24-hour period to do a full-moon ritual. You may not have the space for a permanent altar, or you may not want one permanently filling the space you do have. Temporary altars are also a tasty idea for those who have to keep their witchy stuff under their proverbial (conical) hat. If discretion is needed, a temporary set-up can be the perfect way to feel you've got a witchy HQ without getting rumbled.

If you have a permanent altar, you can borrow items from it for your temporary set-up. Don't forget to take a photo of it if you'd like to remember it in the future. You can even use the photo as an altar in itself! Get the image up on a computer screen or print it onto paper, and sit in front of it as though it's there in front of you. Uh-huh, works like a charm!

Travel altars and hidden altars

Imagine taking a little set-up with you when travelling to visit people or going on holiday. Sounds cute, right? Imagine being able to stash your altar at the back of your wardrobe or pop it under the bed at a moment's notice. Here are some great ways to consider making an easily stored mini-altar:

- Use a make-up or jewellery storage case. I've done this a few times! It's such a fun way to create an altar focal point, because you can stick some images, beads and glitter or other decorations on the inside of the lid and have room in the bottom part for a tea light, a crystal or a flowerhead from your latest walk ... I like to use the storage cases that have a little drawer in the bottom to store a few things, but I've also used a tiny make-up compact that simply opens to an image stuck on the mirror and then I place a crystal or tealight on the bottom half! Adorable.
- Cut out a secret hole in the pages of an old, thick book and pop in some objects and a little cloth for when you need them. Yes, make like a witchy spy, hiding your valuables where no one will think to look!
- Make an altar in a shoebox. You can place all your things inside the box and then have an altar cloth stuck to the lid to act as the bottom of your altar when it's all opened up.
- Keep a few bits in a little bag to get out and arrange in a mini-altar formation at a moment's notice.
- Keep an image on the wall. On its own, it would cause no suspicion and takes up only wall space. Leave the other relevant objects around, such as an incense burner, candle, statuette or bouquet of flowers. When you're ready to do your working, grab all the stuff and bring it to the picture to quickly create your temporary altar space.

- Fill a folder on your computer with images you'd like to use as your altar focal point. When the time comes to do your working, simply go to the folder, find the appropriate image and have it as the screen backdrop.
- Create a beautiful piece of focal art on the back of a shelving unit or chest of drawers. When you need to set your altar up, pull this piece of furniture out so that the incredible altar backdrop is revealed. Then simply pop a few items on the floor in front of it and you'll feel like you're locked back into your witchy home. Then the furniture goes back again when you're finished.

Mind altars

I have a permanent altar that lives in my imagination. I call it my "mind altar" and it contains everything I need to perform magick and ritual, but its existence is non-physical. If this is something that appeals to you, I can't recommend it enough. It's really come in handy for me when I'm away from home and can't sit at my physical altar. It's also great for when my back injury has flared up and I need to do healing magick or a soothing ritual but can't sit at my physical altar because I'm in pain. Ingenious, right? It's all in the mind. If you're wondering how a non-physical altar can have any meaning or even longevity, don't forget that Tolkien had the whole *The Lord of the Rings* trilogy in his brain before he wrote it down. It was obviously intricately mapped out up there in his mind! So many gorgeous details fixed into place to create a living breathing universe that so many millions of people have been wholeheartedly invested in since it was published. Now, I'm no Tolkien, but I'm the world-builder when it comes to my own practice; I've constructed my mind altar and visited it over time so that it's become a solid part of my practice.

If you don't like to use the word "imaginary" for your non-physical tools, experiences, etc, then you could choose to use the word "astral". The astral plane is a place beyond material existence in which mythological creatures, deities and concepts from the world's spiritual systems reside. You could see it as a non-physical location packed with all the spiritual ideas and entities that have made an impact on humanity through time. Although I've read some descriptions of the astral realm that supposedly map it out clearly, I believe it's massively subjective. People who visit the astral realm are accessing spiritual messages and seeing spiritual stuff unfold, but it's going to look and feel different depending on who they are and what they're looking for in there. For instance, not everyone will see angels in the astral. Not everyone will witness the same levels or areas that others talk about. Some people will feel they benefit from their experiences in the astral, while others will return feeling perplexed and unsure of what they can gather from what they saw and felt.

I also feel that it's not always helpful for me to discuss the realm where all the spiritual stuff is kept as being *outside* and away from me. I prefer to think of it as a place that's ultimately *inside* me, but which I have in common with everyone else. I see all the spiritual concepts, beings and experiences that we know about as a species as being a part of what Carl Jung called the Collective Unconscious. It's a deep-rooted part of the human experience that we can all access. For this reason, I tend to prefer to use "the imagination" when discussing places that I visit or things that I create in a place beyond the physical. To me, the imagination is the place in which *everything* non-material is housed, so that's what makes sense to me, but you may feel differently and – no surprise here – that's totally fine!

So, how do you make an altar in the realm of your imagination? Well, as with a physical altar, you can choose to erect something temporary or permanent depending on your needs. I find I'm capable of returning to the same set-up and location many times, but if that's not the way your imagination works, that's fine. My permanent imaginary altar is mounted on a red platform in the middle of a reservoir and can only be reached by boat. There's a large structure over the top from which different trinkets and ribbons hang down. The contents of the altar change slightly each time, but there's always a deck of the same Tarot cards. On my different visits, I've found different bottles on the altar containing medicinal potions for me to drink. I've also occasionally found the altar covered in jumping frogs! Some of the things I experience at my altar are pre-planned and some are unexpected.

Here are some of my key tips for the development and maintenance of witchy spaces within the imagination:

- By all means, brainstorm what you want to create in the imagination. But also leave room for the unexpected to happen. Sometimes you'll be surprised by how your imagination shapes the altar space or what it brings to you each time you visit.
- Go through the exact same considerations listed earlier in this section for the creation of physical altars, applying the points to your imaginary altar-creation process.
- Remember that you can be ostentatious and wildly far out with imaginary altars! If you have limited space in your physical reality, make your imaginary altar huge! If you want a dozen altars but can't have that in physical reality, you know what to do – make it happen in the imaginary realm. Your altars can light up, they can talk, they can have robot hands, they can read your mind ... whatever you fancy, it's a possibility in the imagination.
- Consider having a guardian or two around your altar. I have three Dobermanns watching over mine, as they've always been guardians for me in dreams and magickal workings. I've also created other places in my imagination that have big stone gargoyles placed overhead to keep watch. These are flourishes and not necessities, though!

WRITE IT

◊ Create a timeline of your use of the imagination, starting with any early memories that you have of games you invented or things you made. You may want to include daydreams, fantasies and recurring worries that you visualize in your mind's eye. As you write out your timeline, what do you notice about your relationship with your imagination and how it has progressed?

◊ Describe your ideal altar if money and space were no object. What kind of aesthetic would it have? What would it have on it? Where would it be located? What can your answers to these questions tell you about which components and aesthetics you find empowering and useful?

◊ What is the value and meaning of having an altar space? How highly do you prize the concept of a witch's altar in your own practice? Explain the reasons for your answers.

TRY IT

◊ Sit in front of your altar space and assess your emotional response to it. Which feelings come up? What, if anything, surprises you about this exploration?

◊ Experiment by adding one or two things to your altar that really don't represent your tastes or witchy beliefs. Choose random things if you want, like kitchen utensils or trinkets that don't hold meaning for you. Or select pieces of art that you don't vibe with. Leave the altar like that for a few days and lean into the feelings that come up. Sometimes it pays to step outside of any rigidity around what is aesthetically pleasing or meaningful.

◊ Set up an imaginary altar in a location featured in a favourite video game, book or movie. This is such a fun exercise, believe me!

◊ Struggling to keep the imaginary altar in your mind's eye for long? Try creating a map of it on a piece of paper or in a digital format. Choose where everything on it is located. Look at the map when you need to get the features and layout in mind. You can also simply look at the map or put your finger on it instead of closing your eyes to imagine it, so that you feel connected to the shape and the location of objects as you imagine working with it. People's imaginations work differently so do what works for you. You can also use a photograph of an altar that you like, simply imagining that it's yours and you're doing a working there while you look at the image.

13

SPELLCRAFT

A spell is a formula, usually involving a combination of words and actions, and often utilizing symbolism and correspondences. The formula can be used to shape an event, influence an outcome or promote a particular vibe or attitude. Spells can be designed to harm or to heal. They can increase or diminish the presence of something; they can starve an ideology or promote it. You can design a spell for protection, inspiration, strength, courage, joy, abundance, ability or beauty. You can work a spell for yourself, for someone else in your life, for a whole group of people or for the entire world! Spellcraft is often geared toward external results, such as acing a job interview, passing an exam or finding a great romantic partner. But *internal* growth can also be the focus, such as healing from past trauma, letting go of disappointment or leaving a bad habit behind. A spell can be uniquely designed for one use or it can become a staple template, used by a witch over and over again, tweaked to suit different situations.

Your spells are magickal workings. This means you take the intensity of your desire and your intention to reach that desire, and direct all that potent energy toward the outcome you want. Your desire fuels your vision, turning it into reality.

Things to Consider Before Casting a Spell

One thing you might want to do before writing and casting a spell is to think about your intentions. What is the desired result? Once you've worked out what the aim is, you can decide if that aim is the best possible one. Is it actually healthy? Just because you *can* cast a spell for something doesn't mean you *should*. Lean into your self-knowledge and your chosen witchcraft ethics – they will guide you when you're unsure.

A spell can have multiple aims, but it's probably best for a magickal working not to be weighted down with too many desired outcomes or things can get *confusing*. It's hard to put the power of your desire into the envisioned result if said result has a ton of different components to it. So, be clear and decisive on what you're after before proceeding.

The reason for a spell can be pretty much anything. Here are some examples so you can see the range of possibilities:

- To bring a set amount of money into your life by a specific date.
- To end a long-standing bad habit.
- To enforce a new positive habit.
- To get some great clients and awesome reviews for your business.
- To protect and strengthen a community that you're part of (or an ally to).
- To bring in new career opportunities.
- To feel generally more vibrant/strong/carefree/sexy [insert-adjective-here].
- To protect yourself and your home from spiritual or earthly threats.
- To ensure a good outcome for a project or mission.
- To heighten creative inspiration.
- To improve your overall sense of self-esteem/self-love.
- To connect with a deity or spirit guide.
- To remember and understand your dreams (and make them more informative).
- To make cats like you more.

- To get better matches on dating apps.
- To have the ability to connect with a deceased loved one.
- To strengthen your ability with a sport/maths/art [insert-activity-or-subject-here].
- To get more invites to social occasions.
- To experience less pain/fatigue.
- To achieve fame and celebrity.
- To win a competition you've entered.
- To have more control over your negative thought patterns.
- To heal from your past and finally feel able to embrace the future.

Another thing to ask yourself is whether or not you've taken any *earthly* action toward your desired result so far. The mundane stuff. The real-world stuff. I know, I know, yawnfest. But personally, I'm not the type of witch to cast a spell to find the perfect job if I'm not handing out resumés and applying for interviews. Likewise, I'm not going to cast a spell to find a partner if I'm not on any dating sites, I'm not asking loved ones if they have any single friends – hell, I'm not even trying to smile at anyone at a social engagement. If my spell is saying "yes" while every other action I perform is saying "no", somehow that doesn't make sense. I don't like to work against myself.

Making at least one non-witchy gesture that demonstrates your desire could be an important initial step *before* using spellcraft. This is for a few good reasons.

- Firstly, if you haven't taken any action toward your supposedly strong desire, do you *truly* desire it that much? Maybe friends, family, adverts or social media messages are telling you to want something, but – deep down – you don't really care for it? Maybe you're telling yourself your life would be better if you achieved this goal, but your heart knows better. You can generally tell what you want most from the steps you take to get it, even if those steps are slow and terrified. So, if there's no evidence of real desire in your actions to date, maybe *rethink* the desire instead of *casting* for it.

- Secondly, well, casting a spell can often be a bit of an effort. Personally, I like to do the whole shebang when I make magick happen, so it's often a case of saving time and energy by seeing if some mundane steps work before pulling out my eye of newt and toe of frog. (I'm being literary here. I do not actually have those ingredients in my inventory.)

- Thirdly, as witches we need to consider if we're simply being lazy if we don't try *anything* earthly and then adopt an eleventh-hour "let the spell take care of it" approach. Even if it were possible for me to replace all mundane actions and efforts with spells, I don't think this would make me the best and brightest version of myself. I don't want to avoid all practical earthly effort and stay in a witchcraft-only comfort zone. I want to challenge myself and do things that scare me. Have I done the eleventh-hour emergency spell thing though? Sure I have, and I probably will again. I'm a *rebel* witch, after all.

These are just perspectives for you to chew on. It's up to you to decide why, when and how often to break out the spellcraft. There's no harm in doing a spell early on in your efforts to achieve/receive something, that's for sure. I'm certainly not telling you that spellcraft should always be a last resort. I'll be honest, although spells take effort, they can also be an immense amount of fun to plan and carry out, and it's good to get some practice in. I've done spells just for the sake of it – to test my ability – and that's been a really useful experience. But I always casted for something casual like, "I'll see an owl in the next three days", or, "I'll find something I didn't realize I've lost and it will make me happy". You might want to consider some casual casts just to test and strengthen your skills.

The next thing to consider is how much of the spell you want to write yourself. There are countless spells in books and on websites for your consideration. Some are flowery, lengthy and chock-full of props, while others offer a more quick 'n' dirty approach. Masterminding your own designs may seem like a no-brainer to a rebel witch, but it's worth recognizing that many witches have reported good results using other people's spells. At the beginning of a witch's journey, it can be hard to figure out how to cook up something fizzy and inspiring, so existing spells can provide a decent starting point – and of course can be personalized. If you don't have some of the suggested tools or ingredients, you can substitute them. If the wording is stale, you can write more spine-tingling sentences that really convey your deep intentions.

Of course, not all spells are *written*. In fact, some aren't even *planned*. A bit of spontaneous emergency spellcraft can be just the ticket in some circumstances. Once, when I was on a bus, I did a protection spell on myself and all the other passengers, as things were getting a bit hairy on the road and I felt it was necessary to take some witchy action pronto. These spells can be just as potent as the ones we spend weeks devising. Don't forget that you can also go "half and half", planning some aspects of your spell but leaving room for unscripted things to happen as you go along.

When you do have the time and inclination to pre-plan some or all of a spell, here are a few other things to bear in mind:

Complexity and timeframe

Spells vary widely in their complexity and execution. Some take very little time at all and others may take several hours from start to finish. How many stages do you want your spell to have? Do you want different stages to symbolize different aspects of the desired outcome? How much time and energy will you realistically need?

Time and date

You could choose a specific lunar phase and maybe consider other astrological activity. Or you could pick a day that's special for other reasons – or just choose one when you know you'll have enough energy and free time.

Pre-spell prep

Eating and hydrating, meditating, listening to empowering music, taking a ritual bath or imposing a break from your phone, laptop and other electronics: these are all good things to do before going into spellcasting mode. You might have your own pre-spell preparation activities. I sometimes like to bring all my stuffed toys into my bedroom from the living room to act as witnesses and allies while I'm spellcasting. I dunno, it just occasionally seems to feel right ... I also put on enchanted jewellery – and sometimes clothing – before casting a spell, so you might like to consider that too.

Materials

Do you need any tools or ingredients for this working? Do you need to order anything in advance? How long will it take to get everything together? If you're following a spell written by someone else or previously created by you, do you now want to change anything?

Words

Are you going to speak aloud during your working? Or will the words be said in your head? What's important to include in the wording? (Maybe exactly what you want and how long it will take to come into reality!) Not all witches use words in their spells, so do you plan to convey your desired outcome purely through visuals, gestures, emotions and your imagination?

Actions

You get to choreograph the spell so that it looks and feels how you need it to. All movements and gestures are your choice and they'll mean whatever you want them to mean. For instance, you might decide that you're going to put everything into the cauldron while saying the words you've written. Maybe you'll then put the lid on the cauldron and hold your hands over it while doing the visualization. Then you might decide to walk around the cauldron three times to seal the spell. And finally, perhaps you'll sit back down and light the ceremonial candle. It's all up to you! Remember, you can cast a spell at your mind altar – you don't need to do any of it physically. We'll get into a few examples later in this chapter so you can see some options for spell structure.

Wanna make it happen, chickpea? Here are the basic spellcasting steps

Once you've done your pre-spell prep to get you in the mood to make magick happen, gather any chosen materials together and place them where sacred space is going to be created. Don't forget some water to keep you hydrated if you reckon you'll be in the circle a long time, and you might also want to have a snack handy for when you've finished.

1 You don't have to create sacred space if that doesn't feel right/ needed, but if you want to, now's the time to do it (see pages 104–6).

2 You're going to be using your own innate magickal power to cast the spell, but you can also summon/invite other kinds of power to give your working a nice kick in the knickers. If you work with deities, ancestors, spirit guides or icons such as rock stars, you can request their presence and assistance. You can draw on the powers of nature, identifying specific sources such as the moon, the weather or the elements of earth, air, fire and water. You can try calling on fictional characters from your sacred texts. Or, if there are powerful stories, songs or pieces of art that you feel mesh well with your spellcraft intentions, call in their energy/spirit. I once called on the energy of Gustav Klimt's painting *The Kiss* when performing a healing spell for my relationship. Smashing results.

3 Now it's time to raise energy for your working. If you feel like you're as ready as you'll ever be, you might want to skip this step.

But I always feel like I can go bigger, to be honest, so I raise energy even when I already feel super empowered and ready to cast. This is where you're going to get *passionate*. The powerful energy you raise is going to be gathered up and poured into your desired outcome, so make it count! You can try:

- Dancing, drumming, singing, humming, swaying or chanting.
- Putting some music on and feeling into its themes and energies, letting it fuel you with belief, motivation and potency. I love a bit of black metal or minimal techno, personally, depending on the type of spell I'm doing.
- Visualizing powerful energy inside you and all around you, growing and strengthening, changing colour, and being there to support you.
- Using prayer beads, going through them as you repeat an empowering word or mantra, such as "I fire the arrow of my spell toward my true desire", or "I am a witch, powerful beyond measure, and my will is sacred".
- Spraying yourself with a perfume that smells empowering and let the fragrance symbolize your readiness to do the work. You can also use incense or a scented candle.
- Imagining something powerful and inspiring, leaning into that visualization. A raging sea is a good one, or a strong animal running through its natural terrain.
- Doing a guided meditation for empowerment/strength.

4 Once you feel sufficiently fizzy, you can begin your spell. You might want to start with an opening statement, expressing your desire and reasons for the working. Then, say and do whatever you fancy saying and doing to symbolize your desire coming into reality. As you do whatever you've decided on, *really* focus on what you want and how much you *insist* that it happens. Think about a time when you wanted something so much and you felt absolutely determined to get it. That's the kind of outlook and energy you're going for as you move through the symbolic acts and words that represent your aim. Spells usually have a beginning, middle and end, and we'll explore this below with some examples. By the end of the working, you should feel that you've sent the desire-fuelled energy into your aim, willing it to become reality.

5 Now the working has been completed, it's time to thank the powers that you called in to help you. If you asked a goddess to oversee and protect your working, express your gratitude to her. If you called in a servitor that you made for the purpose of ensuring strong magickal workings, tell it to have a well-earned nap and take the rest of the night off.

6 After spellcrafting you may find you feel spirited and sparkling, filled with the fizzy magickal bubbles you shook up to add to your working. That can be lovely but also a bit weird when trying to step back into the world beyond the circle. So, if you still feel charged by that magickal energy, you could consider:

- Doing a calming visualization where you imagine your energy gently settling or cooling down. You might want to play some soothing music while doing this.
- Earthing your leftover magickal energy – literally directing it into the ground beneath you to be absorbed into the floor.
- Redirecting the energy into one of your tools or your altar space in general, by holding your open hands over the object and feeling the energy run down your arms and drip off of your fingers to be absorbed.
- Using it! Maybe you want to stay fizzy so you can use that energy to do some cleaning or paperwork, do a workout or have a phone call with someone you've been

meaning to chat to for a while but never seem to have the time.

- Gifting it. You can do this by asking an individual in advance if they would like your magickal energy remnants when you've finished doing a spell. Or you can gift it as an offering to an ancestor, icon or deity that you work with, or donate it to a person or group that might need it, such as a nearby women's shelter or a friend with chronic pain who's often fatigued. You could try saying, "I send this energy to _____ to be used in the service of their visions and for their absolute highest good", or "I send this energy to _____ as a gesture of thanks for their wisdom and guidance".

7 Now you've dealt with the bubbly stuff, you may feel the need to reconnect with your body and get acquainted with consensus reality again. For this, you might want to eat something. Energy bars, fruit, nuts, chocolate, a bun/pastry or a sandwich are all good options. Take some sips of water too. You may also want to see this time of eating and drinking as a toast or celebration, marking the work you have done. If you like this idea, consider something special beforehand. If any beings helped you with your work, you could break off a piece of food and bury it outside or burn it in your cauldron as an offering of thanks, or you could pour some of your drink on the ground outside, into an offering bowl or onto your altar cloth to be absorbed.

8 If you created a sacred space at the beginning, you can now close it (see page 106).

Creating Your Own Spells

You can really explore the far reaches of your imagination when designing spells. Don't be tempted just to follow someone else's formula. Writing your own spells is top banana for strong results. There's no witch inspector to check your work and sign off on your spell designs. The only thing that matters is to create something you feel is strong and meaningful and this will give your spell the best possible chance of working. If your ideas seem totally different to anything you've read or heard about, that's probably all the better. If you're simply going to lift spells from websites and books without feeling any form of emotional attachment to the ingredients, words and actions, you're not likely to be bringing all of yourself to the act of spellcasting. You're going to feel detached from an act that's supposed to be fuelled with your focus, intention and desire. It's all about making the spell your own, using symbolism and references that make sense to you. And of course you can mix the traditional spellcraft components that appeal to you with more inventive stuff from your unique brainbox.

When it comes to the words you choose for your spells, feel free to use language in all the ways that make sense to you, and ditch anything that doesn't feel right (no matter how many times you've seen it used in spell examples in books and on websites). Choose word combinations that appeal to you, either because they impress you and you like the sound of them, or because they're words you use often so they feel comfortable and authentic. For example, if you're casting a spell to bring beauty and harmony to your new home, maybe you want to use words that reflect those things for you. I would probably choose something like this:

"I bless each room in my home with the shimmer and glitter of beauty.
Each ceiling, hallway, stair and door is now threaded with harmonious vibes.
Each colour, texture and object revives my spirit and lifts my vision.
Let this home be a place to dance, to sleep and to create –
a palace of protection for me and mine."

SPELLCRAFT

I usually like to finish my spells off by saying, "This is the will of a witch's heart. Let it be so." I dunno, it just works for me.

You might not like any of this stuff at all, but that's great because even if you don't know what kinds of spells you do want to write, at least you know what doesn't flick your switch, so that's a start. Finding your way of using language is a process. Enjoy it rather than being frustrated by it.

For me personally, rhyming sentences always fall flat so I don't try to write spells that way. I also don't use much archaic language – no Ye Olde English vibes for me, thank you. It doesn't come across as authentic and I end up distracted by how silly it sounds coming out of my mouth. If I want a spell to have a powerful punch, I look for linguistic inspiration before writing anything. I listen to artful hip hop and spoken word poetry. I read aloud from books of quotations or prayers. I spend a while looking at the online thesaurus, finding synonyms to replace words that I'm playing with but seem to lack the power or edge that's needed. If I do these things, I tend to write more satisfying spells. Try these ideas if you want to up your game with the way you use language in spellcraft. The bottom line is this: If you want your spells to sound like quirky nonsense poems, that's fine. If you want your spells to sound like they're coming out of a bold, assertive rap battle, go for it. If you like flowery, floaty language that sounds pretty and ethereal, let yourself write spells in that style.

If you're feeling stuck with writing a spell, it might help to break it down into three parts:

Part 1: Declare the intention and symbolize the problem

In Part 1 of the spell you might want to confirm verbally or visually whatever it is that you're going to change. You could lay out some objects that visually describe what you're seeking to bring in and then say some words over them to declare your intention for what is to come. For instance, a red string around a poppet could symbolize heartbreak that you intend to heal, Tarot cards could symbolize a family issue that you want to deal with, and an unlit candle could symbolize the perfect job.

Part 2: Focus on your desire and fully lean into your power

Part 2 is your opportunity to get your desire into your heart and mind. Focus intently on how much you want it and will it to happen. You can do this while visualizing, chanting or drumming, and speaking high-powered words to command the change to happen. Following on from the examples in Part 1, now is when you cut the red string from the poppet, add more Tarot cards to symbolize the positive change you're bringing into the family dynamic or light that unlit candle. Remember, while you're speaking and/or taking any action during Part 2, focus on your desire and your power to make it a reality.

Part 3: Give it a powerful send off

If you think of Part 1 as the lighting of a fuse and Part 2 as the fuse burning down – well, Part 3 is the explosion! This is the point in the spell at which you can give it a good send off. Lots of witches like to do this by saying some woo-woo words to confirm that the intention has left the building and is officially on its way into reality. As I mentioned above, I like to say, "This is the will of a witch's heart. Let it be so". I find that those words just give the whole shebang some extra-strong muscle. You don't need to use words, though. Maybe you could choose a hand gesture, noise or body movement that symbolizes you sending the magick where it needs to go. For some magick-makers, the preferred send-off is a good old-fashioned orgasm!

You can arrange your spell designs so that they hang onto this three-step framework if you like, but feel free to deviate from it, too.

Types of Spellcraft

As you examine spells in books or online, you'll recognize different themes and techniques as they come up time and time over. There's nothing wrong with tried-and-tested kinds of spellcraft, such as candle magick and poppet magick. They're popular for a reason! But you can always change things up. This list of different spellcraft themes to consider should whet your witchy appetite.

Moon magick

The phases of the moon are each invested with different meaning. Although many witches would agree that the full moon represents completion and abundance, while the dark moon represents fresh beginnings, you can feel into the phases from a personal place, deciding what they mean to you. Whatever phase the moon is in, you can call on its intense power, letting the waves of lunar goodness fill you and directing them into your working. Experiment with doing spells during different phases depending on your witchy intentions. You can use lunar energy to protect, guide or empower others in your life, to shield your projects or fuel your dreams. (The same can be said of the energy of any natural or man-made phenomena. For example, you can call on the energy of an abandoned house, a flock of geese, the element of water or a sports car ...)

Candle magick

A candle could represent your burning desire to attain a goal. So, a burning candle could signify your progression and success – as it burns, you get closer to victory. Equally, a candle could represent the light of understanding. As it burns, you call realizations to you, uncovering the truth as the light shines.

The candle itself could also represent something you no longer want – something you're saying goodbye to as you use your witchy intentions to decrease its presence in your life. I've used a candle to symbolize pain I was feeling about a past relationship. I chose a candle with 30–40 hours' burn time, carved it with rune that represented healing and release for me, and placed it in the centre of my altar. Each time I lit the candle, I journaled about the pain I'd been through and sent healing energy to myself and the other people who were involved in the situation. The candle burned down as I did my important healing work, and when it finally burned out, I genuinely felt it had been a magickal guiding force for accountability and inspiration.

A candle in a spell can also represent a person. If a candle represented you in a spell, what could that symbolize? Your freedom from the darkness of heartbreak? Your ability to shine light where there is darkness in the world? Your attractiveness, shining to call in a suitable partner?

Poppet magick

Poppets are often small figures/dolls made out of wax, felt, paper or other materials, although they can also be heart-shaped, animal-shaped and so on. You can purchase them pre-made or create your own (see pages 119–20). As with a candle, the poppet itself can represent you or another person. Pour lavender heads all over the poppet to represent peace and calm coming into your life. Place a symbol or crystal on the figure's throat to heighten your ability to speak your mind. Tie strings around the poppet's arms and then cut them to symbolize you or a loved one becoming free of a shitty situation.

Cord-cutting

This is a type of release magick that acknowledges the ties between yourself and a person, home, job, mindset or whatever it is that you're still attached to. The continued attachment could be caused by your own emotional investment, or the other person's, or the seemingly persistent energy of the situation despite your attempts to free yourself from it. You can visualize the cords being broken during the spell, or you can use objects to represent yourself and whatever you want release from, connecting the objects with string or ribbon that you then cut with your athame or a pair of scissors.

Glamour magick

You could view this as the most commonly practised type of spellcraft because countless individuals and brands worldwide use the art of glamour to get the results they want! A glamour spell changes the way people perceive you, either subtly or radically. There are so many ways you can do glamour magick. Wearing enchanted perfume, jewellery or clothing is one. Changing your movements, gestures and speech patterns is another. What about channelling the energy of a rock star or an iconic actress, or even of an entire historic era or genre of music? Glamour magick is about figuring out what you want to exude and then stamping the hallmarks of that onto your beingness.

This type of magick isn't just a "glow-up", although that's part of it. The greater work is shifting the whole energy around you and fully allowing people to lean into what you want them to feel and assume about you. While you could see this as a deceitful form of magick, I only use it to exaggerate existing qualities of mine or make me more visible and appreciated in a specific situation. Even if you're interested in making others think something about you that isn't actually the case, you could put a time limit on the glamour so it only lasts until after the event or other challenge you're facing.

Sigil magick

A sigil is a symbol that's created to represent a desire – essentially it's the logo of your desire. Each sigil is uniquely assigned to the aim you want to achieve at the time. You can make a sigil by writing out your desire in a full sentence on a piece of paper, taking out all the vowels and any repeating consonants, and then fashioning the sigil out of the remaining letters by putting them into an interesting composition. I often prefer to make a little collage or an abstract symbol that symbolizes whatever I want to cast for. You can go as far out of the box with sigil-making as you like – it doesn't have to involve drawing. For example, you can make an audio sigil by recording your voice on your phone, and then listen to it over and over. Or you can create a dance routine as your sigil, or use a GIF or a selection of emojis.

Once you've designed the sigil, you then kind of fixate on it, connecting with its meaning and pouring energy and focus into it. This allows it to become buried in your subconscious, where it will begin to influence you and guide you into alignment with your desire. It will steer you toward opportunities and away from trouble/failure.

Give your subconscious a chance to grasp hold of the sigil's appearance (or sound) and meaning, then do something to "charge" it. This basically means you're going to programme it with power and intention. You can do this by looking at the sigil while chanting, singing, drumming, dancing, exercising, deep breathing, masturbating, having sex with a partner, or anything else you can think of. Once you've charged it, it's time to destroy the sigil. Tear it up, burn it or delete it. It has been committed to your subconscious and will now begin to shift your behaviour and move you toward your desired outcome in all kinds of ways you're not even fully aware of. The sigil has become a part of the machinery of you – a little SatNav to guide you.

Sex magick

The energy built up from the sexual act can be super potent (obviously). Many witches have used the orgasmic state to direct intention toward their aims, whether that state is achieved alone or with a partner. You can focus on your intention or a symbol of it (such as a sigil) during the sexual act. A partner doesn't need to know what you're doing, but it may be advisable to let them know what's up if they're likely to find a change in your behaviour disconcerting. Also, if they're into witchiness, they could be thrilled to provide you with some orgasmic fuel to get your magickal stuff done!

Tarot magick

Grab your deck and choose cards to represent yourself, your obstacle and your desired solution and result. Lay the cards out and visualize yourself moving through each of the things they represent. You can also speak aloud as you follow the story outlined by the cards, telling the tale of your joy and success. Tarot cards can also be used as talismans of protection or power. Place a card on your altar and call its energy into you or take the card with you into a challenging situation. Visualize a particular card when you're going through a challenge, evoking its meaning to give you strength.

Elemental magick

The four elements of earth, air, fire and water are often considered to be a powerful symbolic quartet that can be brought to mind or used literally to bring about magickal results. You could bury a seed in earth to represent growth or surround yourself with small rocks gathered from the ground to symbolize protection and strength. Air could carry your messages and intentions into the world – send them on incense smoke or in your exhalations. Fire could burn a piece of paper on which you've listed all the things you want to eliminate from your life, or be used to light the way for someone who's lost. Water could cleanse, heal or clarify – bathe in it or pour it over something.

Mask magick

Wearing a mask can be like taking on a new role. Once in character, you may be able to summon or do things you hadn't been comfortable with before. Mask magick could involve making/purchasing a mask to represent a deity that you work with, allowing you to evoke the deity's qualities and then perform magick under that powerful influence. Or a mask could represent a particular characteristic that you have, allowing you to tap into it more fully when the mask is over your face. Or it could symbolize your future self; once you're wearing it, you can enact what you intend to do, sealing it into a prophesy for yourself.

Banishing

This is "be gone" magick. In other words, when you want something or someone to go away and *stay* away, you do a banishing spell. Banishing can be heavy-handed, but the risk of an excessive result can be minimized by using precise wording and gestures that stipulate the outcome you're really looking for. Plus, who's to say that there aren't situations in life where someone or something seriously does just need to be banished? No judgement here! You could use a biodegradable poppet and bury or burn it to symbolize the disappearance of the person, project or situation. Maybe you'd like to have a servitor or deity briskly escort someone or something from your life, or form a protective barrier around you so that the offending person/situation can't get too close. Or you could decide to do a visualization in which you boot the troublesome individual over a rainbow or rip a project into pieces and throw into space.

Binding

If you need to "save someone from themselves", you can do a binding spell on them. And yes, you can do one on yourself if you're being your own worst enemy! Binding is less severe than banishing. Rather than getting rid of a troublesome person from your sphere altogether, a binding will magickally disarm them so they can't cause any further injury. A classic way to perform a binding is to take a photograph of the person causing a ruckus and use cloth or a ribbon to make a bandage around the image, representing the sealing-off of their behaviour so they can't inflict pain or cause trouble anymore, and may also begin their healing if they feel inclined to do so. You can also do this to a poppet representing the person.

Hexes and curses

OK, first of all, the definitions of these words are a bit fiddly, so let me get that out the way. The words "hex" and "curse" both describe some kind of action that brings ill-fortune, misery or harm into someone's reality. Technically, the word "curse" doesn't necessarily suggest that witchcraft has been used. Non-witches use the word, too, for instance when they claim to have been cursed by fate, cursed by God or to be struggling with a family curse that runs down the ancestral line, affecting those with the same DNA. "Hex" is the witchy version of this – to hex someone is to put some kind of unpleasant spell on them.

However, I've noticed another set of definitions being used for these two words among witches. A curse usually denotes something more savage and lasting than a hex, the latter being a working that brings in a period of bad luck for someone or invites a specific unfortunate event into their life. Hexes are usually designed to wear off eventually and may be created intentionally as a short, sharp lesson to teach someone something. A *curse* is more extreme. It may even be life-long or multi-generational, affecting the children of the person you lay it on!

Poppets are often used to get specific about the effects of a hex or curse. For instance, a classic technique is to use pins to select the locations of pain, physical or mental, and stick them into a poppet representing the unfortunate recipient. Someone who wants confusion and disarray to enter a person's life might spin the poppet around and shake it, talking to it in gobbledegook or taking it out into a strong wind or snowstorm. If the desired result is for the person to lose something that's dear to them, then a stone, Tarot card or other object can be used to represent what will be lost. A witch might tie this symbolic object to the poppet and then cut the tie, visualizing the sadness that will be felt when the loss occurs. Another way of hexing or cursing someone includes writing a magickal story, full of relevant detail, in which the individual experiences misfortunes. This can then be read aloud in sacred space while the witch visualizes it all coming true. Creating a servitor to cause trouble in someone's life is also a possibility.

Hexes and curses are usually doled out as punishments for bad behaviour. You may want to hex an ex-partner who betrayed you, reserving curses for extreme situations such as abuse. Make no mistake, hexing and cursing are controversial in the witchy world. But the decision is ultimately yours – it's your practice, after all. While some witches feel that balance is restored naturally when someone does a shitty thing, others feel that witchcraft is an obvious way to create justice for wrongdoing and they have no qualms about getting their hands dirty in that department. (See pages 215–16 for some of the ethical considerations when deciding whether to hex or curse.)

MAKE IT HAPPEN

Protection magick

Following on from hexes and curses, now might be a good time to remind you that protection and shielding are totally a thing in magick. You can shield your property, your body, your creative project, a friend in need or a whole community. Visualize the subject of your protective energy being surrounded by high-vibe white light, or physically encircle a symbol of whatever it is you're protecting with salt, crystals, moon/storm water. Speak words of powerful guardianship over the object. Let your intentions for the safe and fortified future of the object of your protection be super-strong!

Blessings and cleansings

Sometimes the energy around a person, place, object or project feels a bit yucky or cluttered and it's time for a cleanse. The concept of cleansing energy explored in the Spiritual Hygiene chapter can definitely be applied to spellcraft. You can cleanse energy back to neutral or raise it so it feels more hopeful and positive. Chase away energies that feel obstructive or scary, and bless whatever you're cleansing, giving it your witchy seal of good fortune and high vibrations.

Art magick

Your artistic creations can serve many purposes in spellcraft. A piece of art could be a talisman against failure, sadness or unforeseen obstacles. Or it could represent a being you want to get closer to or an aim you want to achieve. Or it could be enchanted with all kinds of good energy and then hung on the wall so that all who pass by soak up its lush vibes. Plan your pieces super-strategically to call in specific results, or let your imagination and instinct decide what the art will deliver into your life. Gleefully destroy your art by fire when it's done its job if you like or, if you prefer, keep it as a reminder of power and possibility. You can also gift magickal art to loved ones after imbuing it with positive intentions for its intended owner.

Stitch magick

Customize your everyday garments to transform them into magickal tools. From sewing a label marked with a sigil into the back of your jumper to decorating a coat with enchanted beads and sequins, your magickal clothing can form part of a daily routine of empowerment and protection. Clothes can also be used to send out certain messages and energies to others, so that you can find friends, attract potential partners or ace your job interview, etc.

Energy gifting

Have you ever noticed yourself stepping into a room full of people and transforming the mood with your high vibes and excited energies? It's amazing how infectious your optimism and good intention can be! When you consciously decide to deliver positive vibrations into a tense or lacklustre situation, you offer your own mood and intention as catalysts for collective upliftment. This works well in strained or high-drama work environments, and it's also great when you're around a loved one who's dealing with stress.

Memory magick

Find safe places in the tapestry of your past where you can hide your secrets, cook up your ideas and take the time to reconnect with yourself. Could you revisit your favourite hiding place from childhood, perhaps? Or a beautiful holiday location that always makes you feel positive when you bring it to mind? You can also visit the memories that still hurt you and scatter healing intentions all over them. Think of memories as locations that provide you with evocative settings for transformations to take place.

Story magick

Creative writing will help you bring your desires to life. Scribble your fizzy visions down on paper or tap them into a document on your laptop/phone. As you write, feel the willingness to see your desires materialize and let that willingness fill the story with the magickal power to make itself come true. Read the finished story aloud in sacred space for best results. You may choose to work with very short stories that take place in different settings with fresh characters each time, or write an on-going manuscript featuring one story with the same locations and cast of principal characters.

Magick playlists

You can collect songs to describe a goal you want to achieve or a feeling you want to experience. Let yourself discover new tracks or just include those that already pull on your heartstrings or fill you with the urge to take back your power. Music is a deeply shamanic prescription and a carefully created playlist, designed to put you into a certain mood or fill you with inspiration, is sure to be a majestic tool for change. Listen to the playlist in its entirety while visualizing your success or put it on shuffle to give the cosmos a hand in shaping your spell with sound.

Food magick

Putting an enchantment on food gives you the ability to ingest physically your own magickal intention. The enchanted piece of fruit, energy bar or bowl of pasta then turns into a high-powered magickal object that can be eaten to release its potency. Don't forget that putting a spell on food to be eaten with others means that everyone will receive the benefit of the magick and your intentions for the group. You can also enchant long-life snacks and nibbles so they can provide you with whatever you might be missing in a moment of need. A bag of sweets in your car's glove compartment can be enchanted to release feelings of calmness and control for when you're feeling stressed on the road, for example.

Fiction/game magick

We're often emotionally connected to films, books and video games, investing hours of time in these other worlds, so their potential for working magick should not be overlooked. You can banish bad energies to a location from a beloved book, draw power from a specific powerful movie scene or use a scene from a video game in a symbolic way to represent something you're aiming for in your life. For instance, why not use a racing game as a way to magickally symbolize yourself getting free of your current situation/location/relationship and moving on to something new?

Internet magick

Specific word searches, websites, memes or emojis can be associated with different aspects of your magick. Maybe sending a certain emoji sends a particular energy into the recipient's life. Maybe you could choose a specific website or channel to visit in order to stock up on a certain emotion. If you think about it, many people do watch a certain type of video or follow specific hashtags when they want to feel a particular emotion. They're already working magick on themselves – they just don't think of it that way and perhaps therefore don't fully and deeply take advantage of it.

Keep adding to this list, learning lots of other magickal techniques. Experiment to discover the kinds of spells that really flick your witchy switch. Remember that you can combine two or more spellcraft types. For example, you could design a spell that uses Tarot cards to symbolize different situations or people, and involves lighting a candle that you've dedicated to your desired outcome and watch it burning while listening to a magickal playlist. Smash the different magickal ingredients together in a colourful recipe of witchy wonderment, honey bee!

WRITE IT

◊ Make a list of adjectives to describe how the act of spellcraft should look and feel in your practice. There are no right answers here. The words "elaborate", "glamorous" and "mysterious" are as appropriate as "chaotic", "messy" and "bohemian". Your spellcraft, your way, your rules – or lack of them.

◊ Which spellcraft types/ideas would you like to try in your practice and what would you use each one for? Choose from the list above and elsewhere, writing down your reasons for your choices.

TRY IT

◊ Surf the internet to find between two and five spells of any kind – for love, money, work or whatever ... it's up to you. Take a look at each spell, deciding what inspires you about it and what isn't so crash hot for you. Then switch up different aspects of each spell until they all really pop!

◊ Design a spell that is somewhat out of character for you and do it. Check the results. Going outside your comfort zone can be a good way to evolve in your practice and find new techniques that you like.

RITUALS AND OTHER WITCHY ACTIVITIES

A ritual is a high-powered act that holds great meaning. Unlike spells, which call in specific results, rituals tend to be more about acknowledging and honouring what *is*, rather than seeking to *change* it. Although funnily enough, when you perform a ritual, interesting transformations *can* happen – usually transformations in your own perspective or emotional outlook. This is because rituals invite a deeper sense of acceptance of the reality you're experiencing and the feelings you're going through. They therefore lessen any resistance or denial that was making an issue harder to cope with.

Spellcraft allows you to bring in what you desire, but that's not always necessary. Sometimes you may recognize that your desire is not possible or healthy. In that situation, a ritual may enable you to accept what's unfolding rather than desperately hanging onto the hope of changing it. A ritual may also be preferable to a spell if you're just not sure what you ought to be casting for. Perhaps you're waiting on more information before deciding if you should cast a spell or not. During the delay, a ritual can help you prepare for unknowns and feel calmer and more capable. Rituals can be performed to help you with all kinds of things, from accepting truths and releasing tension to processing tough emotions and getting ready for something new.

Don't forget that our lives are already filled with all kinds of rituals that convey meaning and help us to process life's events. Cultural and religious rituals that symbolize feelings and intentions at times such as birth, coming of age, marriage and death are common. There are rituals associated with graduating from university, winning a sports match, getting a job or moving into a new home. Families and friendship groups develop all kinds of rituals that are carried out during the dinners and conversations they share. And personal rituals are as power-packed as they are commonplace. Maybe you have little things that you do for luck, for example, or to help you make a decision or brighten up your weekly commutes to work. Ritual is the psychedelic thread that runs through the tapestry of life to make it more colourful and interesting. In consciously designing and performing a ritual as a witch, you are acknowledging how important ritual is to human beings and taking that meaning and richness to the next level.

In witchcraft, you may perform the same ritual many times through the years as with the non-witchy examples mentioned above. But you can also design unique rituals for one-time use. You may want to use the same ritual each time when you're celebrating the full moon, for example, or as part of a devotional to your chosen goddess. But a one-time ritual written from scratch may feel appropriate for saying goodbye to a home you're moving out of or marking the end of a friendship. Each time a ritual is necessary, you can decide if you want to create something new.

Rituals don't have to be planned out meticulously and rehearsed beforehand, although it's fine to approach them that way if you want to. Some rituals may come to you more organically and you may flow with the moment, allowing things to develop unscripted. Some of my favourite rituals have been slapdash and spontaneous. But yes, I've also spent hours designing rituals and had everything written out to follow step-by-step as I went along. It really depends how you're feeling and what seems necessary each time.

RITUALS AND OTHER WITCHY ACTIVITIES

Types of Ritual

Let's have a look at some types of ritual so you can see the possibilities. As always, this list is not exhaustive. There's so much more out there and [pointing to your forehead] in *there*.

Celebration

If you want to acknowledge something that's truly made a difference in your life or the lives of others, ritual helps you to do so *deeply*. Celebration rituals can include reading a statement of thanks (with or without a toast), playing some relevant cheery tunes, singing and dancing, or munching some delicious celebration cake. Yes, you can do all those things and more in one ritual. Go wild with it.

Worship

This type of ritual allows you to adore, appreciate and show respect for a deity, ancestor, icon, location or even the entire planet itself. You could make a speech, make an offering or create a piece of art to symbolize your adoration and thanks. Whatever comes to mind and feels appropriate is fine and, yes, you can totally design a ritual of worship for *yourself*. Don't let anyone tell you differently!

Dedication

If you'd like to move into a closer relationship with a being you've been working with or learning about, you may want to dedicate yourself to them. This type of ritual symbolizes your commitment, showing that you intend to learn from the being in an ongoing way and perhaps also give regular offerings or otherwise be in consistent contact. You can also do this kind of ritual when you want to commit to a regular practice or course of study, or commit to abstaining from an unhelpful habit. Earlier in the book I mentioned consecrating objects to use in your witchcraft. Consecration can be seen as a form of dedication in the sense that you are dedicating yourself to the inclusion of the object in your practice and to learning from it or putting it to good use.

Healing

If you or someone around you has been injured or unwell, a ritual could symbolize readiness for healing and belief in that possibility. You could ask any beings you work with to watch over the healing process, visualize healing occurring or perform some symbolic actions that symbolize healing. If you're doing a ritual of healing for yourself, you may want to bring in things that usually feel healing for you, such as music you enjoy listening to or food, such as herbs, with relevant healing properties.

Emotional expression

If you know it's been difficult for you to process and release your emotions fully around a specific topic, ritual could help. I personally like to have "pillow screaming" rituals. I know it sounds super-odd, but if I stick my face into a pillow and just scream for a while at the top of my lungs, I tend to feel much better about whatever is aggravating me and I feel I've exorcized a lot of anger and frustration from my system without the neighbours hearing me and calling the police. Fashioning this into a ritualistic context feels really good. I also allow myself to write unsent letters that externalize any anger I feel. I imagine the person I wrote them to standing in front of me, and read them aloud. Usually, I end this ritual by burning the letter in my altar, but sometimes I prefer to seal it and put it in my altar drawer, to be opened in the future when I'm ready to look back from a totally different point in my life.

Journey/pilgrimage

Rituals that involve an imagined or real journey can be super-fizzy and meaningful. You may want to visualize a journey to the land of a deity you're working with, or to your ancestral lands to meet with your forbears. You could visualize a journey to a certain part of your psyche that requires healing or attention. You might want to journey back to a certain point in your memory in order to make your peace with that time. Think about what the journey is intended to achieve before carrying it out. Journeys in the physical realm are also appropriate for this kind of ritual. You could visit a forest, maze, spiritual site or other focal point, such as a statue in a stately home, moving around it as part of your ritual. Journeying around a gallery or museum could represent a pilgrimage to symbolize thanks, inspiration or personal growth.

Self-honouring and self-care

Ritual can help you celebrate your progress and acknowledge how far you've come. You could pour yourself a glass of champagne or eat something delicious, or make a speech highlighting your achievements or qualities. You might want to get dressed up nicely for self-honouring rituals. Take some selfies and pictures of the ritual set-up to commemorate the moment. For self-care, run yourself a bath or read your favourite book under a blanket in your pyjamas. You can use a poppet that symbolizes you, if you like, applauding it as you read out its achievements or tucking it into bed by swaddling it in a blanket and singing it a lullaby.

Preparing/welcoming

Maybe you're getting ready for something, such as a new home, child, job, business, project or pet. Or perhaps you're preparing for a significant event like a party, a funeral, a first date or one of those crunch-time conversations you sometimes have with a loved one or colleague. Whatever it is, designing a ritual to put you into readiness is a great idea. These rituals may include cleansing your energy or space to ready it for whatever is coming. Decluttering and organizing may be part of the ritual, too. Perhaps you'll want to read out some commitments or choose some words/objects of power that symbolize your willingness to move into this new experience.

Releasing and goodbye

When you know you need to walk away from something or someone but perhaps are struggling to understand *how*, ritual can help you set yourself free. I once selected a Tarot card to represent the person I needed to leave behind. I spoke to the card as though it was that person who'd wronged me and been unkind. I poured my heart out to the card, imagining the person in front of me. I then went to every other room in my apartment and out onto the balcony and then into the street, spending time away from the card and imagining that each hour I spent was a full year away from that person's influence and the pain they caused me. After midnight, I went back to the card and I felt a completely different way about the person that the card symbolized. It was a very powerful goodbye ritual and by the end of it, I knew I could release that person from my life. I put the card back right at the bottom of my deck to symbolize burying the connection and having a funeral for it. I then cleansed the deck and that was the end of the ritual. Other good ritual acts for saying goodbye include writing a farewell letter or listening to a playlist of songs that symbolize your impending freedom.

Life change/rite of passage

Acknowledging that life's events change and shape you as a person – or that you *want* them to – is a great reason for ritual. Think of any change that has significant meaning for you or that you'd like to see as a turning point, and design a ritual to mark it. Gender reassignment, moving to another country, ending a relationship, arriving at menopause, reaching retirement, selling your house or hitting a milestone of any kind are all great examples of times when you may want to perform a life-change ritual. During the ritual you could change clothing or accessories to symbolize the shift taking place in your life, or read a passage from one of your sacred texts that symbolizes empowered change. There are so many more options. Let yourself be inventive.

Sabbat

We checked out the eight Sabbats on pages 50–7. Rituals to recognize a Sabbat could include all kinds of things from dance, chanting and visualization to speeches, offerings and consuming relevant food and drink. Connect with the themes of the Sabbat you want to celebrate and see what comes to mind for you. Don't forget that you can totally make your own set of Sabbat days or put an entirely different spin on the existing ones.

Birthdays, anniversaries and various holidays

In order to reclaim the direction and energy of birthdays, anniversaries and holidays such as Christmas and Easter, you may want to carry out a ritual that puts your own spin on the proceedings and allows you to embrace an authentic way of celebrating. This can be great for witches who are often forced to compromise on how they'd like to recognize key events. How would you like to celebrate your birthday in a ritual? I often do so by carving out sacred space and spending an entire day making sacred art dedicated to my goddesses and spirit guides, and to myself. I've also gone on ritual walks during annual public holidays, symbolizing my independent perspective on the meanings of such events and reminding myself that I'm always coming from a position of sovereignty and that I don't have to do anything just because society tells me to.

For Christian holidays and traditions particularly, you could look into which elements of these actually stem from pre-Christian customs (if you don't know about this already, you'll be pleasantly surprised). You can also create your own rituals for baby-naming ceremonies and funerals. Witchy weddings are often referred to as "handfastings" and you can find tons of ideas for them online as well as figuring out how you might personally want such a celebration to look and feel.

———

You can begin your rituals by cleansing the energy and creating sacred space if you want to, just as you might like to at the beginning of the spellcasting process. Likewise, you can ground energy, have something to eat and close sacred space at the end of a ritual. But there's no obligation to do any of that. Anything can happen in any order – go with how you feel and what's meaningful to you. It's also worth noting that any ritual can include a spell within it, which is quite cool. The ritual is kind of wrapped around a spell like a chocolate with some tasty liqueur in the centre. But there's no need to include a spell within a ritual. Many of my own rituals do not include any intentional change-making act. They simply honour what is, and that alone can be exceptionally powerful.

WRITE IT

◊ Human life is studded with the shiny jewels of rituals – some regular and some once-in-a-lifetime. What would human existence be like without these many rituals?

◊ How has ritual featured in your life in the past? What about now in the present? And how do you intend for ritual to feature in your future?

TRY IT

◊ Compare the experience of a pre-planned ritual and a totally spontaneous one. Think of a theme/purpose for the ritual first. Then, begin to design your pre-planned version. Carry it out and reflect on it in the days afterwards. Then it's time to do a totally spontaneous one based on the same theme/purpose and spend some days reflecting on that before eventually comparing them. Which one was more powerful and why?

◊ Consider a ritual that you often partake in. It can be a Sunday family dinner, a good-luck ritual, a self-care routine or an action that you take to begin or end each week/month. How can you make this ritual more witchy in nature? Tweak the ritual to make it feel like an act of witchcraft and consider the results.

Other Witchy Activities

So, what other witchy treats are on the menu? It's not all about spells and rituals. (Thank goddess, because that would be tiring!) Lots of the other activities that you might want to do during your dedicated witchy time – from meditation and visualization to mirror work and affirmations – can be included in spellcraft and ritual, but they are standalone actions, too. You may find that you spend the majority of your time doing this other witchy stuff, to be honest, since most witches try to avoid overkill when it comes to spells and rituals. I personally don't know many witches who do a spell or ritual, like, every single week. (But hey, this book is called *Rebel Witch* for a reason, honey – do what you feel and don't let me tell you what to do.) These other activities don't usually require any preparation – you can just start doing them right away, any time. So, whereas you might feel the need to take a long run up to a ritual or spell with energy cleansing, creating sacred space and/or raising energy, the following activities are generally more low maintenance.

Meditation

Meditation can help you to be in the moment, be at peace with yourself and experience life more fully. It's also well known for helping to sharpen mental focus, making it an obvious training activity for magick-makers.

There are many different meditation techniques available. I personally like to use guided meditations and listening to binaural beats. I also like to repeat words of power while handling one of my many sets of prayer beads. There are many good books on the philosophy and theory of meditation if you want to dive deeper and get better at it over time. Meditation challenges you not to get too fixated on anything that you are imagining or worrying about. When you are meditating, you simply acknowledge any thoughts, feelings or memories but ultimately try to let them go and stay in the flow of the now.

Visualization

Whereas meditation challenges you *not* to get too fixated on anything that you're imagining or worrying about, visualization challenges you to hold a vision in mind and commit to it totally. There are many guided visualizations that you can follow, or you can decide upon something to visualize. I've sometimes recorded my own voice taking me through a visualization of my own design rather than following someone else's, and I must say that it worked like a charm.

Cleaning, cleansing and organizing

If you have an altar space, there will be times when you want to cleanse it energetically and/or physically clean it. You'll also want to change the cloth, rearrange the items and so on. If you're working with a mind altar, you can still do all these things, but you can be more inventive with the technicalities. Maybe your new altar items will be brought to you on the backs of glittering unicorns. Or you could throw no-longer-wanted altar tools into the sea where they'll dissolve like bath bombs and new tools will be magickally born from the foam of the waves.

Practising and preparing

When you're not doing life-changing magick and deliciously deep ritual, you can be getting ready for it. Planning to use your crystal ball or Tarot cards in your next ritual? Well, you might want to get some practice in beforehand. Writing some words for a spell you'll be doing in a few days? There's no time like the present to get that wording as potent as it can be. If you want to make a spell bag, you'll need to collect herbs and plants from your garden or source them from a shop.

Doing a reading

Some witches like to pull a Tarot/oracle card or a rune for themselves each morning, noting down a key message to take into the day with them. You can do this daily if you like, or weekly, or as it suits. Of course, there are many ways to do a reading. You can scry if you like, or simply request and receive messages from a deity, guide or other being. (Divination is explored in full in the next chapter.)

Praying

Some witches aren't keen on the word "pray". I quite like it these days, but I grappled with it in the past and it's fine if you'd rather use a different term. What I mean by "pray" is that you can commune with Divinity in any way that feels comfortable for you. I sometimes talk to my chosen goddesses, asking them to be with me through the day, give me answers or guide me appropriately where needed. I thank them and tell them my problems and then just sit in their energetic presence. Many people do this with their ancestral spirits or spirit guides. You may want to ask Divinity or a chosen being for answers and then write out whatever comes to mind, or record your voice speaking the sacred words flowing out of you. Sometimes I pray by simply gazing into my own eyes in the mirror on my altar, witnessing the Divinity within me and honouring that.

Mirror work

This is a powerful technique for self-development and healing. If you can't or don't want to use a real mirror, you can imagine looking into one or choose an object that represents you at the present time in your life. Gaze at yourself and say words of love, empowerment or encouragement to be absorbed into your heart and mind. This practice can help people to get through tough times and learn more about themselves. I also just like to speak the truth into my mirror, even if it's harsh or scary. It helps me realize what the root of a particular problem might be and that in turn helps me understand what next steps might be necessary, both magickal and mundane.

Journaling

Using loose paper, a notebook or a document on your computer or phone, you can write about all kinds of things. Write about your spiritual path in your witchy journal or jot down notes for the next spell or ritual that you're planning. Write about your emotional healing journey. Make a gratitude list or a list of the things you want to learn next on your witchy path ...

Devotionals

If you work with any kind of being, or simply with the energies of the planet or cosmos, you can perform a devotional. This can include speaking or writing words of thanks and praise, giving an offering and confirming your commitment to your relationship with the being.

Affirmations

An affirmation is a statement that promotes strength, inspiration or healing within you. You can find lists of them online or try writing some of your own. Affirmations can help you tune into your aims and harness your best qualities. Try writing them or speaking them aloud. Some good examples of affirmations are:

- "I love, accept and appreciate myself, and will always protect my interests."
- "I choose to exercise and eat well because I care about my physical health."
- "I refuse to allow people to bully me or breach my sacred boundaries."

RITUALS AND OTHER WITCHY ACTIVITIES

Drumming, singing and chanting

Sound, rhythm and repetition can be therapeutic. For many witches, drumming or singing has a calming and/or strengthening effect, and can be just what's needed to prepare for spellcraft and ritual – or simply get ready for daily life. When you sing or chant, you can choose to use words that have deep meaning for you, songs you've loved for years, time-honoured chants and mantras, etc. But don't be afraid to make things up, too. When you're drumming, simply focus on what feels good. Get that rhythm and consistency going and lean into the flow, letting it change organically as it wants to or in accordance with something that you may be imagining in your mind. For instance, if you're visualizing yourself running down a hill, you may want to match this by starting to drum more quickly.

Tapping

Emotional Freedom Technique, aka "tapping", is a process in which you tap certain points on the body while repeating a series of sentences a number of times. The sentences are customized to your needs each time. Tapping is supposed to help people free themselves from negative habits and harmful mindsets, and many who use it claim it's very useful. Learn more about this simple but effective process if you feel that it might aid you.

Study and research

Whether you're interested in herbalism, mythology, Tarot, astrology or witchcraft traditions from different cultures, make time to hit the books and trawl the internet in order to enhance your witchhood. If you're studying for a certification of some kind to help you with some aspect of witchcraft, don't be tempted to delay the work you've committed to. You can find courses in crystal work, meditation, ritual and so much more. Check out the student reviews and testimonials before enrolling if you're not sure which course is right for you.

Getting creative

Your artistic pursuits will naturally overlap with your spiritual endeavours. Dancing, singing, playing an instrument, painting, writing stories or poetry – the list goes on ... As a rebel witch, you can certainly take the combination of creativity and witchiness as far as you want it to go in your practice. It's not just about using art and music in your spellcraft and ritual. For example, you can make art to decorate your altar, to represent the beings you work with or to help you with emotional healing, shadow work, etc. (See Chapter 19 for more on shadow work.)

Helping someone

Being of service is an important focus for many people on a spiritual path, not just witches. Thinking of others and helping to make reality better for all rather than only focusing on the self is a fairly obvious spiritual pursuit. Decide whereabouts you most want to help out and put some money, time or energy into the causes you care about. Give food to your local food outreach programme, offer some of your time to volunteer or consider how you could use your skills to help an individual, a charitable organization or the planet itself. Your energy and power can really make a difference.

It's important that you don't push yourself to give too much. Everyone has different capabilities and limitations depending on what is going on in their lives. You may sometimes be able to give more than at other times and that is totally OK. Sometimes we're in survival mode and we need to reduce our efforts until we feel stronger. Think about what you can do rather than comparing your efforts to others or pressuring yourself to achieve something that isn't realistic right now. In particular, don't offer money that you don't have or exert yourself way beyond what you know is healthy.

Sleeping, cooking, working out, making love, watching movies, organizing paperwork or chatting with a friend on the phone ... all these can be seen as part of your witchcraft routine too. Most mundane activities can be injected with the witchy vibe, approached from a witch's perspective and fuelled with witchy intention.

RITUALS AND OTHER WITCHY ACTIVITIES

WRITE IT

◊ Take another look at the list of other witchy activities suggested above. On separate pages, jot down all the items you've already included in your witchy path or plan to very shortly. What's the true value of each of these activities? What excites you about each activity? What isn't so great about each one? Try to put as many thoughts on each page as possible.

◊ Again using separate pages, write about the items on the list that don't appeal to you and that you don't currently intend to try. Why are you not so taken with these activities?

TRY IT

◊ Choose one of the other witchy activities that really doesn't appeal to you and – you guessed it! – try it once to see what it's like. Were you pleasantly surprised? Or were you right to think it wouldn't exactly make your cauldron bubble over? (Obviously, darling, please don't try anything that would be unhealthy/dangerous for you.)

◊ Choose an activity that you regularly do and consider mundane and non-witchy. Try bringing a more magickal approach to it, including when you're preparing for it, when you're carrying it out, and afterwards. What was your experience of making this everyday activity into something more witchy?

15

DIVINATION AND COSMIC GUIDANCE

Many of my most supremely witchy times have included divination – the act of using a spiritual tool or practice for the purpose of receiving guidance and understanding. When I'm open to answers from beyond the ordinary channels, I feel so connected to my power. Although I like to weigh up the pros and cons of decisions in terms of practical considerations, I also know that this process has its limits. Sometimes I want a strong spiritual sign that confirms the conclusion I'm coming to in my rational mind, so I use divination methods to welcome that kind of spiritual input. If I have an uneasy feeling about something or someone and can't put my finger on why, divination helps me out immensely. And if I don't feel tuned in to the wonderment that's all around me, a powerful divinatory experience can change that. Some of the messages I've received through my Tarot cards or crystal ball have convinced me that there's more going on in the universe than we can really explain and that we're all wired up to a greater wisdom that goes beyond the rational and the material. This belief is at the heart of my witchhood.

Divination is commonly seen as synonymous with fortune-telling, and there's no doubt that many witches do use divinatory methods to find out what the future is likely to hold and what the probabilities of different outcomes are. But you can do a range of other things with divination including:

- Plan strategies for projects and events
- Solve everyday problems
- Choose between two or more paths
- Heal emotional wounds
- Receive calming messages when you're worried/stressed
- Confirm your suspicions about something/someone
- Spark creative inspiration
- Choose your priorities or the order of business
- Receive guidance from beings such as deities, spirit guides or ancestors

How to Do It

When using a divinatory tool to receive answers and insights, you can choose a specific question that you'd like the tool to help you answer, or you can select a broader focus area to explore. For example, a question would be something like:

- How can I find more friends in my area?
- Why do I keep running into the same issues in my romantic relationships?
- Where should I go on holiday?
- When would it be best to sell the house?

And a focus area would be something like:

- Finances
- Relationships
- Creativity
- Health and fitness

Focus areas are great when you want to explore something but you're not sure what your queries are or what you want to know. Questions obviously work better if you know exactly what it is you want to know. Of course, you don't need either a question or a focus area when you practise divination. It's perfectly fine to use a divinatory tool just to see what kinds of messages come through, without directing the reading in a particular way. Sometimes you might choose to leave a reading open to whatever may need to come through for you. Such open readings can be intriguing and powerful.

Before we explore a tasty menu of ways to practise divination, here are a few points to consider:

Consider timing

You may pop some spontaneous divination into your day for no other reason than you feel a need for it in that moment. But you also have the option to schedule divination so that it coincides with your birthday, anniversary, a specific lunar phase or other astrological event, and so on. Sometimes saving a specific date adds meaning and anticipation into the mix. You could schedule divination to coincide with a Sabbat, so you're drawing on the Sabbat's themes to help you receive useful messages. You may also want to schedule divination for a time of day when you won't be disturbed and you'll have ample time to receive the messages and sit with them for a while.

Make it fancy

There's nothing wrong with quickly pulling a few cards on a whim or sitting down at your crystal ball for a no-frills divination session. But giving the occasion a bit of ceremony may help you take the guidance in more fully and give it a feeling of deeper meaning. You could light candles, burn incense and put a special cloth down, laying symbolic objects out to represent your questions and intentions. You could also make the divination session into part of a bigger overall ritual. Maybe start things off with some words to state your readiness to receive the insights and your commitment to following the guidance. After the divination, you could do some meditation, chanting or journaling.

Think about your beliefs

If you're not sure exactly what you believe about divination, that's OK. Some believe that the received insights come from the gods, from the energy of the universe or from spirit guides who seek to give you advice and warnings. Some believe that the messages are created by the unconscious mind, which shapes them in a meaningful way so they are relevant to your life. It is possible to believe both these things. You might like to take some time to think about your own theories. What is the power and meaning of divination, from your perspective? What is happening when you receive shockingly accurate or significant messages from divination? How closely will you pay attention to the messages you receive? Do you think that all guidance you receive from divination should be adhered to? There's no pressure to know these answers, but you might want to have fun considering them.

Lean into your gut instinct

Second-guessing, overthinking and rationalizing won't do any good. When it comes to messages you receive during divination, try to value your deep instincts and inklings. Pay attention to what you feel like when you go with your gut and try to welcome that feeling into your divination practice as much as possible. We sometimes try to defy or ignore our gut instinct because it's not something that can be rationally explained and it may seem unreasonable or silly. But hindsight can often show us that our instinct was right on the money. This reassures us that sometimes we just deep down know something even if we can't explain how. There's no shame in having a hunch about something. If you get those kinds of hunches while working with a divinatory tool, honour them and pay deep attention to them. They are not a mistake.

Prepare to be confused

There could be times when the guidance received during divination doesn't make sense to you. It can be frustrating when this happens, especially if you're in a hurry to get the answers you want so you can solve a problem or make a decision. A bit of time and distance from the reading might be needed, though. Take a breather and then come back to the messages and consider them again. You may find that you were overlooking your answer.

Types of Divination

There are literally hundreds of divinatory practices to choose from. Some require the use of a tool, such as a deck of cards, a set of runes or a crystal ball. But many don't involve a material object – all you need is your mind. Check out all the options and pursue the ones you feel drawn to. Here are some for your consideration:

Tarot and oracle cards

The 78 cards of the Tarot provide amazing guidance to help you make decisions and see possibilities. If you don't feel attracted to the complex Tarot system, there are lots of oracle card decks that you can choose from instead. Oracle decks tend to be simpler and come in an endless variety of themes, whereas Tarot always has 78 cards broken down into four suits with more defined meanings. Once you have a deck, you can design big card spreads in which every position answers a different question or addresses a different theme. Or you can just draw some cards more randomly and feel into the combination that has come up. Many decks come with guidebooks to help you understand what the cards mean. But of course, you can combine the official meanings with your own intuitive interpretations. You can even get a pack of playing cards and collage over them to create your own deck with your own meanings.

Palmistry

The bumps and lines on the hands are different for every human being on the planet. This is why it's so tantalizing to appreciate how the "maps" provided on your palms may give you a sense of where you're headed, what you will learn and what your life is all about. All forms of divination provide room for your individual interpretation. However, there's a lot of consensus around the meanings of the lines of the hands and there are names for each set of lines, so you can research that stuff if you want to learn. In fact, you can interpret all kinds of marks on the body, from hair patterns to mole positions. I've often wondered what the triple six under my hairline means. Only joking.

Scrying

Most people have practised scrying by looking up at the clouds, pointing and saying, "That looks like a deer's head", or "I can see a house". But while most people leave the observations there, a witch considers the symbolic meanings of the observed images and how those meanings might apply to situations in the witch's life. You can scry using all kinds of tools including crystal balls, scrying mirrors, tea leaves, bodies of water, stretches of sand, candle flames and incense smoke. You can even use the darkness behind your closed eyelids. Don't be afraid to get creative. I once scryed using my partner's hair when they asked me for advice on how to promote growth in their life. (I thought that one was quite clever.) I've also scryed by throwing a bunch of my clothes onto the floor and reading the shapes they made when they landed. You can seriously do it with anything.

Runes/Ogham

Runes are a collection of ancient Norse symbols, rather like an alphabet. You can purchase a set of runes that are painted or carved onto wood or stone – or make your own, if you like. Shaking the runes in a bag and scattering them can be a good way of seeing what is coming up or what kinds of actions you can take to solve problems. As with Tarot, the individual runes have meanings that you can study and memorize, and you can mix those meanings with your intuitive sense of what they're trying to tell you when they come up in readings. Ogham – the Celtic equivalent of Runes – is another symbolic system that you might want to check out and learn.

MAKE IT HAPPEN

Pendulum

You can purchase gorgeous pendulums made with all kinds of crystals in teardrop shapes. But you can also just use a set of headphones or any necklace with a pendant, or make your own – tie a string around a small object, such as a stone, and you've got yourself a pendulum. Hold the string still, letting the object attached to it drop into the air, and swing. There is meaning in the direction in which it swings and how rapidly. You might decide that barely swinging at all means "do nothing for now", whereas rapid or exaggerated swinging means "take immediate action". Swinging from north to south might mean "the person you're dating isn't right for you", whereas east to west means, "the person is a good match". Or you could place some objects or words on the ground and see which one the pendulum seems to be swinging to. I would recommend deciding on meanings for the pendulum's behaviour *before* setting it to swing so that you can't be biased about the results!

Reading behaviour

If you have a pet, you can observe its behaviour, deciding in advance the divinatory meaning of certain actions it might take. Let's say your cat is eating food from its bowl. If the food is finished entirely, what does that mean? If the cat wanders away and leaves some food in the bowl, what does that mean? If you have a dog, take it for walk and decide that different forms of behaviour will mean different things. If your dog meets another dog and gets along with it, what does that mean? If your dog runs after a stick but doesn't return it, what does that mean? You can read human behaviour too, and the behaviour of vehicles on the road and so on. What is the symbolic meaning of a traffic jam? The symbolic meaning of a delayed flight? What about the meaning of seeing two people having an argument? Of course, you probably don't want to think in this predictive way about *everything* you witness, so you can put a time limit on it. You can decide that the way your pet behaves on one particular morning is your divinatory tool, or the way your family act at dinner will tell you something.

Numerology

Numbers and number combinations have different symbolic meanings. They also have meanings that are personal to you, such as your current age, your house number and your lucky number. You can study numerology in depth if you fancy incorporating it into your list of divination methods. To find numbers that give you guidance and understanding, try using an online random-number generator, or closing your eyes and tapping a calculator, or flipping through a book and noting the page numbers wherever you stop. You can also pay attention to numbers you happen to spot, such as on posters, when glancing at the clock or in a reference number of a purchase. Tarot cards are numbered, so you can read the numerology there, too, if you use the cards.

Automatic writing

Set an alarm and keep writing, typing or talking into a voice recorder until the alarm goes off. Don't overthink and don't plan. Just keep the words flowing. The aim is to get out of your rational mind and through the urge to decide what the words are going to be. Then read back over the randomness that you wrote and look for the divinatory meanings. You could also take this approach to dancing, recording yourself and then watching the footage, or to painting – or any other creative activity.

Random generators

There are online random generators for numbers and all kinds of other things, from book titles to drag-queen names to suggested hobbies. I also think of the shuffle feature on music apps as a type of random generator. I like to go to a gigantic playlist and hit the shuffle button – the song that starts playing is the one that's offering me answers and guidance. Try it!

Bibliomancy

Close your eyes and flip through a book, stopping whenever you feel called by a certain page. Run your finger down the page to get to a specific sentence or just decide that the entire page holds divinatory meaning. You can do this with picture books as well as with text-only books, and with online articles and blog posts. An alternative method is to fast forward through a film or video, pause at random, then read the meaning of whatever happens when you press play.

———

You can choose different divinatory methods for different situations. I often use runes to receive messages from my matron goddess because she's a Norse goddess, so that just really feels like it makes sense. For messages outside of deity connection, I like using Tarot and oracle cards, or scrying with my crystal ball or with incense smoke. Sometimes a particular divinatory method seems more appropriate or convenient. I like to do playlist-shuffle divination when I'm deciding what to do with my day off because it's fun to see what comes up and the result is quick.

When you decide to use divination, you obviously have something in mind that you're actively questioning. But sometimes cosmic guidance comes to you suddenly, without a request from you, so don't forget to value that seemingly random stuff. You may find that you have a dream that contains interesting symbolism or seems otherwise meaningful. Maybe you could research the objects and events that featured in the dream to see if that turns up any answers, or simply interpret them using your intuition. Or, you may find that a pattern keeps occurring – perhaps you hear people using the same phrase in different situations and you feel it's a sign, or you see the same theme coming up, the same colour everywhere, a number that keeps repeating. This kind of synchronicity can have great significance. The more you are open to it, the more you can feast on it and feel fed by it. (If you don't feel that a pattern is significant, that's fine.

Sometimes there's an obvious reason that you keep seeing a pattern and when it can be logically explained, you may feel that it doesn't have deeper meaning – it's your call.)

WRITE IT

◊ What has your previous experience with divination been? Don't forget to consider any divination you may have done in childhood without knowing it, as well as any times that someone else did divination for you.

◊ What would the world be like if everyone used divination to make key decisions and solve problems in their lives?

◊ What are your aims with divination in the next few months? Where would you like to see progress or try something new?

TRY IT

◊ Experiment with a form of divination that you haven't tried so far. How does it go?

◊ If you're ready to use divination for others, try offering it to a loved one and seeing what happens. Get feedback: what did they think of the guidance and information you offered? In particular, ask them what they appreciated about it and why. This will help you ensure that your practice improves. If they have any constructive criticism for you, try to implement it.

MAKE IT HAPPEN

main recordkeeping device by whatever term you like, but for the sake of ease, I will use the acronym "BOS" here. The BOS is where you can record your ethics and aims as a witch, as well as your witchy calendar, plans for rituals and spells, and the outcomes of past workings. You may also want to write up your research in your BOS, record your witchy activities, and keep lists of things you want to buy or try. You can also record encounters with beings, prophetic or symbolic dreams, experiences of synchronicity ... the list of possibilities goes on.

Grimoire

This is a more formal type of BOS – less personal, more presentational. Grimoires are common in covens where they are a shared record of arcane wisdom, passed from witch to witch to learn from. For solitary practitioners, a grimoire can serve as a reference book containing the solid knowledge that has been acquired. A grimoire doesn't usually contain anything super-secret – it's not for intimate details and insights, but tends to be a bit more "official", containing only material that will be repeatedly referenced as part of the practitioner's personal lore. (And some witches just like to use the word "grimoire" in place of BOS, because, well, grimoire is a fucking cool word.)

Book of Mirrors

This is more of a witchy journal to hash out thoughts, feelings, dilemmas and possibilities in a long-winded way. Whereas a BOS may contain the ingredients, components and outcomes of a spell, a BOM is more likely to contain a lengthy write-up of how you *feel* about the spell and its results. A BOM may have a confessional nature, so it's often a deeply personal tool containing your most profound feelings about the witchy journey.

Dream journal

Many witches keep a separate dream journal and like to analyse their dreams for shreds of the future, information about their own feelings or visitations from beings offering insight. For those who remember their dreams and find repose to be eventful and interesting, a dream journal can be indispensable. For a witch who doesn't dream or doesn't tend to *care* about their dreams, it's not at all important. Plenty of witches choose a middle ground and record the occasional dream of significance in their BOM, myself included.

Art/poetry book

You can choose to put any art or creative writing relating to your craft into your BOS or BOM, but you may also consider having a separate place for it. For instance, lots of my artwork pertains to goddess worship and witchhood, so I see my art journal as a magickal tool. I also keep a book of devotional poetry and prayers dedicated to my goddesses, and it also contains the channelled writing that was done when I asked Spirit/Goddess to write through me.

Mood/vision boards

When you need to be inspired or empowered, a collection of visual references can be a mighty tool. Sticking images and words onto a board to create a collage representing a desired mood or outcome is a great way to tune in to the vibe of what you want to bring through. It can also be a way to explore your feelings about a situation or brainstorm something you intend to do. I like to make paper collages using magazines I've collected over time, gluing them into my BOS or witchy art journal, or using pins and a corkboard to make a temporary arrangement. I also like to use Pinterest, and I keep folders on my phone and laptop filled with images to symbolize the specific archetypal energy I'm interacting with or outcome I'm working on. I use these collections of images to fire me up and fill me with inspiration.

Research notebook/folder

If there's something you want to study for your witchy path, you might want to keep the notes together for review and revision. You could keep separate notebooks for different topics, or file papers in ring-binders categorized by subject. You may simply prefer to keep notes from study in your BOS, but I like to keep my study notes separately because they can get messy.

Photo album

You may want to keep records in photographic form. I particularly like to do this to record altar setups as I often change these; taking photos gives me the chance to look back and witness what has been important in my practice over time. I also photograph setups for rituals as well as the spread layouts for big readings I do for myself during Sabbats or at other significant times. Some people share their photographs on their witchy social media accounts, but there's no pressure to do that. You can print your photos out or store them digitally.

As we discussed at the start of this book, there's no requirement to keep physical records. You can use documents on your computer or phone, which will give you the opportunity to edit. You can store voice recordings on your phone or laptop in date order. I personally do prefer to keep written records on paper, but rather than writing in a bunch of different notebooks, I use a ring binder. That way I can keep multiple categories of records in one place and reorder them as I like, recycling or reusing the paper I don't need anymore.

Some witches I know use the bullet journal format for their BOS or BOM. Others use code in their record keeping, either to keep the information sacred or to keep it secret if there's a chance the book will be the victim of prying eyes. While the well-worn trope of a witch writing long-hand in a massive volume filled with delicious witchy wisdom is a glorious one, it's also far from the lived reality of a lot of witches. Many don't have time to keep such detailed records, or they can't afford a book like that, or they find it too laborious to write by hand. There's only one "right" way of recordkeeping – and that's the way that feels right for you.

WRITE IT

◊ What forms and styles of recordkeeping – if any – have you already tried in your practice? Which ones would it be most helpful to learn from and revisit?

◊ Are there any recordkeeping methods that you'd like to try out and why?

◊ Have you felt any pressure or uncertainty about recordkeeping?

◊ How much do you revisit your past witchy records?

◊ How important do you feel presentation is in your record keeping, if at all?

TRY IT

◊ Switch up your recordkeeping habits for one to four weeks, depending on how curious you are to experiment. Maybe you could try adding little doodles/sketches to your BOS to explain things instead of using words. You could test drive a ring binder, if you like that idea. You could increase the amount of journaling/recordkeeping that you do or stop keeping a record of things that feel boring/ pointless to track. Try it and see what works and doesn't work for you.

◊ Try keeping a record in photographs. You could store them in a folder on your phone or on a social media account, or print them out and stick them in a scrapbook. Photograph your altar and ritual setups, the ingredients for spells, shots from meditative nature walks – or whatever you fancy. Add captions if you feel inclined.

Statement of Power: From strong foundations, bold actions and clear principles, my path continues to grow. I reach new heights as I learn and improve. Evolution, triumph and discovery are the rewards of my ongoing commitment to witchhood.

Part III
LET'S KEEP GROWING

Part III is about preparing you to start carving out your own rebel witch path. In Part II, you had a chance to decide on the kinds of things you'll include in your practice. Now you can look at how to weave those things together in your life, creating a schedule for your witchy activities, figuring out your level of flexibility and also learning to recognize when it's time for a change. We'll also troubleshoot issues such as cultural appropriation, toxic comparison and spiritual slumps.

SCHEDULES AND PLANS

OK, OK, I'll admit it, dollface. The title of this chapter doesn't seem very rebellious. This is supposed to be a book about colouring outside the lines and here I am using words like "schedules" and "plans". Before you start yawning and rolling your eyes, hear me out. You are carving a once-in-a-lifetime path for yourself, studded with all the shiny stuff that you love most of all, and that's awesome. However, it can also be an invitation to end up with a messy mish-mash of confusion. If you're worried about life getting in the way, making a schedule can ensure that you get some witchy practice each week/month. Alternatively, maybe you're worried about falling so deeply into your witchy practice that other aspects of your life barely get a look in! Scheduling activities allows you to do one thing at a time and do it efficiently, rather than wanting to do *ten* things at once but doing none of them properly. (Please tell me it's not just me who has this issue?)

A rebel witch is usually a mystical magpie. In other words – you see something shiny and you want it! There might be hundreds of things you want to try, so many doors you want to open, or things you want to study. But if you try to do everything at once, you'll risk burning out. A schedule will help you stick to a manageable number of experiments in your craft.

Witchcraft is a process of discovering what works for you. If you're trying ten different kinds of magick, setting sacred space in five different ways and working with a dozen deities, how will you be able to pinpoint what's making a real difference? With fewer activities on the go, you'll be better able to see what makes your practice pop. Try something and see if it does the business for you. If it doesn't, cross it off the list.

Designing and committing to a schedule is an act of self-discipline, and self-discipline can heighten your self-esteem and sense of empowerment. It's good to know that you can decide on something and stick to it. When you commit to your plans and carry them out, you get to feel responsible and capable, and this may fuel your potency as a witch and as a human being. And your schedule isn't set in stone. Flexibility is not a dirty word. Life takes weird and wonky turns, so it's OK to move things around. Schedules don't have to be long-term. You might just want to create a schedule week-by-week or month-by-month, reviewing the results at the end of each period. At that point, you can tweak the schedule on the basis of what was the cat's pyjamas and what fell flat. If you have lots of activities that you want to try, consider scheduling experimentation periods for them. For instance, you could have a full month of studying Tarot and practising meditation, followed by a full month of studying herbalism and practising mirror work. At the end of each experimentation period, review your progress and thoughts, and decide if you want to change it up.

Scheduling your witchy activities helps you to maximize your time. If you only have an hour or two for witchy activities during the course of the average week, you're going to want to make sure those hours pack a powerful punch. It's OK if you can only engage in witchy activities on Saturday afternoons, or if you just have five to ten minutes for a quick morning practice at your altar each day. Creating a schedule helps you get real about time constraints. Rather than telling yourself you've got all the time in the world and then feeling sorely disappointed when you realize you haven't, your schedule reminds you that it's fine to have only a small window for witchiness, as long as you use it constructively.

SCHEDULES AND PLANS

You don't need to follow a schedule *all* the time. Many witches are totally free and easy, going to the altar when they see fit, performing rituals/spells when the fancy takes them and doing card readings for themselves when the time is right. You might fluctuate between having a schedule and just going with the flow. But if you're only just starting out, or your witchy practice seems to be evolving, a schedule can be a useful tool.

And it doesn't have to be complicated. Maybe you want to set aside just five minutes every morning to meditate or record and interpret your dreams, saving altar cleansing, divination, spellcraft and other witchy stuff for *one* day of the week, when you know you have time. A more rigorous schedule would include activities for morning, afternoon and evening, but if you don't have the time or energy for that kind of busy practice, don't sweat it. Less can definitely be more.

WRITE IT

◊ What excites you about the idea of scheduling your witchy activities?

◊ How could keeping to a schedule of planned activities help you be a more powerful witch?

◊ What are the things you definitely want to include in the schedule? What would you like to include, but can have more flexibility on?

TRY IT

◊ Create a schedule for one week, then try it out. You may want to divide each day into morning, afternoon and evening activities, or keep things simple by just having one sentence/statement to clarify your intention for each day. Is there a Sabbat, Esbat or other event that you want to recognize in this time? (You could journal about how you'll celebrate these events or how you feel after doing so.) If you want to perform a spell mid-week, or meditate every morning, then add that in but don't feel pressured to schedule activities for every day. When the week is done, review the schedule. What would you change?

◊ You might want to upgrade to a monthly schedule. This schedule could have differences from week to week to keep things interesting. One week you could study astrology, for instance, and the next week you could practise scrying. Try it out, then review it and make the changes you want.

ETHICS

Figuring out your personal set of moral principles as a witch can get a bit sticky. It's normal to have strong ethical standpoints on some things while being a bit wobbly on your ethics in other areas. It's also normal to find that your ethics change over the course of your journey. If you're fairly new on your path, don't worry if you don't have everything neatly figured out yet. Your ethics will be challenged by different situations that will arise as you go, offering great opportunities to tighten up or tweak your views. It's better to leave yourself plenty of witchy wiggle room rather than trying to nail all your ethics down before you've even started. And the question of witchy ethics isn't confined to newbies. Seasoned witches may find one of their strongly held ethical principles suddenly being challenged or, as they change on the journey, their ethics may shift. It's always good to check in with your ethics, wherever you are on your path.

Witchcraft helps you to pursue your desires, so it seems sensible to have an ongoing dialogue with yourself to ensure that you're not trampling over other people while aiming to get what you want. One thing I love about witchcraft is that it puts the practitioner's power and vision at the centre of things, encouraging us to use our agency to enhance our lives and the lives of others. But the shadow side of this is forgetting to consider the potential harm of selfish or hard-hearted magick. Many witches find themselves checking their reasons for doing magick and this ensures that their intentions are in an honourable place and they have considered perspectives aside from their own. But one witch's unethical shit-show is another witch's justified action.

The idea of the "threefold law of return" exists primarily within the established witchcraft religion Wicca, but it is also discussed and advocated in other areas of witchcraft, too. This law states that anything you send out with witchy intention will return back to you three times stronger in some form. It deters witches from doing sassy, mean magick that could potentially come back and bite them in the backside later on! Even if you don't believe that what you send out will come back to you threefold, it still pays to imagine that it *might*, if you want to make sure you stay on the right side of your own ethics. "Do unto others as you would have them do unto you" is generally pretty sound life advice, whether you're thinking about whether to cast a spell or simply responding to a situation in a non-witchy context. However, not all witches vibe with this idea, and some situations may prove too complicated for you to follow any rule you've set for yourself.

Throughout your journey in the witchy world, you may meet people who will seek to strong-arm you into their way of thinking. Ethics are personal and intense! If you're unsure what your ethics are, then you might want to hold back on a particular course of action until you're clearer on what you think and feel. But don't be tempted to do something – or not do something – just because you want other witches to approve. This is *your* sovereign journey. Converse deeply with yourself. If your reason for wanting to do something is just "Because I want to", then you may need to accept the possibility of later regret. Thinking things through properly and knowing our reasons is the best route to a long-term sense of peace with what we've done as witches – and as human beings.

It helps to know where the key bones of contention are when it comes to witchy ethics, so let me break some of them down here. This list is nowhere close to being exhaustive, but it's a good starting point.

ETHICS

Participation in other spiritual traditions

You're entitled to duck out of spiritual stuff that isn't directly related to your beliefs. Some witches choose not to attend church, for instance. Others *will* attend but may abstain from parts of the service. Personally, I would attend a Catholic Mass and might quite enjoy the prayers and hymns, but would definitely opt out of taking Holy Communion. It's all about leaning into your own boundaries, discovering where they are and then vocalizing them. A lot of the time, compromise is an important ingredient. A witch who was raised within a practising Christian family may feel that it's worth continuing with the tradition of attending church with relatives when the occasion arises, whereas for another witch that would be unthinkable.

If you're a witchy parent, you may also have to think about how much you want your own spiritual outlook to influence your kid/s. I know lots of witches who enjoy involving their children in events on the witchy calendar, provided the kids seem engaged, and some of them are raising the kids in a multi-faith household so it gets even more interesting! But I also know witches who keep their practice very much to themselves and only discuss it with their children if questions arise.

Using stuff from other cultures

Many different cultures have been denied the right to practise their spiritual beliefs over time. They've had their customs banned and suppressed or treated with derision, and their spiritual and religious artefacts were pillaged by those who colonized their lands. These cultures may find themselves in an active fight to preserve their endangered beliefs and practices, with stereotyping, discrimination and misinformation continuing. When witchy peeps incorporate things from indigenous/minority cultures they don't actively belong to, they run the risk of endorsing such oppression.

Lots of witches do find themselves interested in practices from outside their background, but will make a special effort to be respectful, for instance by ensuring they purchase learning resources created by active members of that community. This ensures that the money goes back into the culture itself rather than simply allowing outsiders to profit from the community's practices without giving anything back. Many witches feel it's OK to learn about a wide range of different beliefs, but may refrain from actively carrying out the practices associated with them, whereas others feel it's fine to incorporate the practices in their own path if they've studied them properly. It's important to find out whether or not a particular religious or spiritual tradition considers itself open to outsiders. Some cultural practices should only be carried out by genuine members of that group and it's deeply troubling for the community when outsiders adopt and publicize the practices. Think carefully about where you stand on incorporating any practices you're not fully connected with and clued up on.

You might want to take some time to consider *why* you want to include anything that comes from a culture or tradition that wasn't part of your upbringing. Is it because you feel this could connect you to your ancestors or to the land you live on? Is it because you find these practices beautiful or interesting, because they resonate with you and inspire you? Are such reasons strong enough? How much do you feel you ought to know about a certain tradition or practice before you can forge an authentic and useful connection with it? A practice that seems interesting in isolation usually has all kinds of associated customs and beliefs that enrich and explain it. Lifting a custom that interests you away from its original context and slotting it into your practice may seem like a creative thing to do, but it's worth asking yourself if there is an inherent laziness or entitlement in that approach.

If a spiritual custom from another culture interests me, I usually try to figure out why I find it attractive and then seek to create something of my own that taps into the same themes while also being authentic to me and therefore much more relevant to my path. It's worth asking yourself if a custom of your own devising would be the more powerful option than borrowing from somewhere else. Building your own lived tradition is an ongoing act of invention. When we simply take from what already exists elsewhere, do we challenge ourselves enough creatively and intellectually?

Love spells

Performing a spell that encourages a person to develop strong feelings for you can certainly be seen as an attempt to override their free will. Consider whether or not you really want to plant seeds of attachment within a person who didn't have them in the first place. Is it fair to exert that kind of control? You'll also need to contemplate the likely consequences of such workings. You may not like the way someone acts once the spell is cast. (If you're thinking of the classic '90s film *The Craft* right now, then you understand exactly what I mean!)

A love working can help you to call love into your life without messing with anyone else's head in the process, and hopefully Part II offered some ideas for your consideration. But ultimately, it's your call. One good way of figuring out whether or not to perform a spell that's intended to change someone's view or make them act differently is to consider seriously whether you'd be happy with someone doing the same thing to you!

Spells for others without their knowledge

You may feel that performing workings for others without their knowledge could never be an ill-advised thing, as long as it's for something yummy such as healing, love or career success. After all, it's benevolent magick, intended to help: what could be wrong with that? However, while many witches do send out magickal workings and witchy intentions to people in their lives, many also refrain from doing so. Others *ask* the individuals before proceeding, to avoid overstepping any boundaries and to make sure the person in question is absolutely OK with it. You'll have to decide where you stand on this.

The thing about doing magick for others is that your own belief in your magickal ability will lie at the heart of its success. If you're really worried about performing a spell to help your friend with their upcoming job interview because you fear that it might backfire, are you really in the best position to cast that spell? Or is it fair to say that your belief in your ability to control the outcome is a little too shaky to make the spell successful? And some would say that over-confidence can be problematic, too, because it stops a witch from considering all the consequences, and causes them to be gung-ho instead of proceeding with caution. Here's my two pennies: if you're not confident enough in your skills to do workings for others, consider just doing them for yourself first. Strengthen those magickal muscles and sure enough, you'll come to feel capable of providing magickal support without fear of unintentionally landing your friends and family in the spiritual shit!

Giving advice/predictions without being asked

As a witch, it's easy to get excited about your keen perceptions of people or situations. Witches tend to have exceptional intuition and can therefore often give strikingly accurate insights into what's really going on under the surface or predict what's coming around the corner. Witches sometimes get messages from beings they work with, too. They can often interpret coincidences and strange happenings in people's lives, tuning into the deeper layers of meaning that others may miss. This is all very tasty stuff, and you'll find yourself becoming better at it – in your own unique way – as you progress on your path over time. But when is it appropriate to *tell* people about your witchy perceptions? If you have a vision of something bad happening to someone you love, should you tell them in order to help them avoid such a fate? If you get a message from a spirit guide and it relates to someone you know, what should you do with that information?

It can be unpleasant and unsettling to receive unsolicited advice. While some may be glad of witchy intervention and insight, others may resent it or be very fearful of it. Consider your position on this. You may find yourself tempted to share your witchy musings, but it's not always the appropriate time and it can cause people to focus more on what you're saying rather than on tuning into themselves, putting you into a position of power over them. One considerate way to deliver information is to ask the person if they'd like to hear your insights before blurting them out.

Binding

When someone is engaging in destructive behaviour or endangering themselves or others, you can take magickal action in the form of a binding spell. Bindings are usually seen as benevolent workings, designed to help someone who seems unable to help themselves. Witches tend to use them when they want to stop someone from doing something harmful, such as abusing drugs and alcohol or engaging in violent behaviour. So, on the surface of things, it doesn't seem like there's much of an ethical quandary here.

In performing a binding, you're deciding that you know what's in someone's best interests – and this incurs the risk of making the wrong judgement call on their behalf. Plus, you're overriding their free will. Some witches see binding as interfering in an individual's journey toward solving their issues themselves in their own time and really understanding their experience deeply. Binding can also be potentially difficult to execute long-term, as in many cases you'd be fighting with an individual's super-strong urges toward destructive behaviour. This makes a binding more likely to be a temporary measure that then wears off as the individual insists on causing more trouble. In a situation like this, is it more sensible to cast protection magick for *yourself* rather than binding the other person? I like to think of protection for me as being more energetically cost-effective in the long-term than a binding spell for another person, plus I bypass the risk of infringing on their free will. This doesn't mean I won't take some kind of non-magickal action to help, such as engaging the troubled person in a conversation or encouraging them to seek help from an appropriate professional.

Banishing

Banishing a person from your friendship circle, workplace or online community via magick is a possibility. If you want someone to disappear from wherever you keep encountering them, a banishing spell could do the trick. But you will be messing with that individual's free will, so you'll need to take that into account.

It could also be said that banishing magick lets you off the hook, in a way. After all, we have to interact with people we don't like sometimes. Is it responsible or realistic to use a spell to get rid of someone without very good reason? Banishing may also disconnect you from some great lessons that you could be learning from interactions with people you're struggling to get along with or who have wronged you. Although banishing magick may be an important aspect of protecting yourself from a bully or abuser, it might not be appropriate for less extreme situations. Ridding someone from your space doesn't necessarily help you to learn how to deal with anything. Instead, it may give you the feeling that anyone who doesn't do things your way should be removed – and that might not be an attitude you want to encourage in yourself.

Hexing and cursing

Using spellcraft to inflict a penalty on a wrongdoer is seen as ethical and as unethical, depending on who you ask. Some witches would say that the scales of justice should be permitted to balance themselves without intervention. Others, I think, would ask what witchcraft is really for if it's not – at the very least – a tool that can be used to hurry that kind of process along. A hex/curse can be seen as an act with great cathartic value for the victim of a wrongdoer. It can be performed so that its only effect on the wrongdoer is that they begin to understand the gravity of what they've done. In other words, hexes and curses can ultimately be about bringing healing and understanding to both parties, with the wrongdoer realizing that they've been a shitty person who needs to change (which may be punishment enough) and the victim feeling that they've had a chance to express their rage and pain.

But, obviously, such justice means creating some measure of chaos, sadness, fear or loss in a wrongdoer's life. So it's fair to say that you should be confident enough in your skills that you can control the severity of the yuckiness that you're sending out. You might also want to ask yourself if you can aim the "justice vibes" in the right direction, so that they don't hit someone undeserving! It's one thing to work with healing intention and end up sending it in a random direction that you didn't intend. But it's quite a different kettle of witchy fish when you find you've directed a curse at someone who genuinely didn't deserve it. Your working could deeply negatively impact a loved one of the wrongdoer, who has done nothing wrong and really doesn't deserve the pain they will experience by association. There's even a chance that the wrongdoer could turn out to be innocent.

Another thing to reflect on when deciding if justice magick has a place in your practice is whether or not you're truly an appropriate judge who can hand down serious magickal sentencing. Do you have a decent perspective on what someone should experience as their just deserts? I know that I can be a bit heavy-handed in that department, especially when my ego's been bruised. I like to imagine all kinds of nastiness befalling someone who's been a dick to me, and for a while I might be convinced that they'd deserve it. Look, I'm a hothead at times, OK? I blame genetics and my natal chart! Deciding to perform a hex or curse usually comes from a place of raw and high emotion. As you're on that rollercoaster of thoughts and feelings, you might just tell yourself you need to bring someone's entire life down, only to regret it later. And by then, it could be too late. I'm not trying to caution you against anything, cupcake. This is your show and you can run it as you please. But it's definitely worth giving some time to this consideration.

Communing with the dead

Many witches work with the dead in one way or another, whether they call on the spirit of a deceased loved one for guidance, perform seances or use a Ouija board. Many witches are guided by spirits who used to walk the earth in human form. They take messages from the world of the dead, to benefit themselves or others. Some witches have had such abilities since childhood and can't actually help connecting with those who have passed over. But some believe that waking the dead for guidance or gain can be bad form or that it can cause big trouble! The notion of working with the deceased outside your own ancestral line is something that some witches don't vibe with either. And while many witches and other mystical types make their living from contacting the dead, others don't even believe it's possible.

Lean into this exploration. Do you believe in contact with the dead? Have you had personal experiences with it? Would you like to explore this area further, and if so, why – and what are your aims? Where are your limits in this regard? Is it OK to try to wake the occupant of a random grave, for example? Is it OK to accept a large sum of money from someone who wants a message from their dead relative? Is it OK to use a Ouija board to see if any spirits come through, or is that something you wouldn't personally try?

Working with demons and death deities

Many witches work with deities, spirit guides, ancestors and other disembodied beings. They glean guidance and strength from such beings, and may also request help from them when performing spells. Deities who preside over death, war or destruction would be totally off limits for some witches, while others have strong connections with them. In the same way, some witches feel drawn to working with demons, while others may loathe the idea. Some may be tempted to work with "darker" beings, but feel it's too dangerous. Keep in mind that witches who work with death deities, demons and other beings of the more shadowy variety are not usually working on malevolent stuff. A demon could help you with success. A death goddess could help you with healing. Just because a being has a bad rep doesn't mean it can only be useful for bad intentions. And just because a being generates fear does not mean it *should* be feared.

Of course, if you personally get a dodgy feeling about the idea of working with a particular being, then don't do it! No one is forcing you to cosy up with Lucifer if you'd really rather not. Some of the ethical conundrum can lie in whether or not you find yourself judging *other* witches for the beings they choose to work with. It can be important to check your biases and make sure you have your facts straight before assuming a witch's intentions and character are tainted by the reputation of the disembodied beings they hang out with.

Taking payment for witchy services

Witches tend to develop a tantalizing skillset over time. Many become practised in herbalism, Tarot/oracle readings, interpreting astrological birth charts and other cool stuff. Lots of witches have abilities such as reading people's auras (energy fields), being able to chat with the dead and, of course, performing spells to bring all kinds of tasty stuff into people's lives. It stands to reason that some witches will want to make their living from the abilities they have – and many do. But it's not a foregone conclusion and earning a living from witchcraft doesn't make you any more (or less) legitimate a witch. Lots of witches don't believe in charging money for their services. Some feel their skills should be given freely when requested because they're gifts from Spirit and shouldn't be used for profit. Others feel that taking money just complicates matters and they prefer to offer their help gratis when they really feel it is needed. And many witches feel that receiving payment is absolutely vital because it denotes respect for the work and represents a fair exchange that promotes positivity.

Of course, when it comes to taking payment, a witch should know their stuff. There's nothing ethical about charging moolah for something you know you haven't really mastered, whether that's carpentry, bakery or witchery! So if you're going to be stacking coins by doing spells or reading cards, it's important to decide if you're truly ready to give your customer a good return on their investment.

Environmentalism and responsible consumption

Awareness about ecological threat and the need for sustainability is becoming increasingly prevalent – and with good reason. Climate change, natural disasters, endangered species and the destruction of the habitats of wildlife and those supporting indigenous people are all topics that have found their way into everyday conversation. Indeed, many witches were conscious of these issues long before they were hitting the mainstream headlines. Witches tend to work closely with nature's cycles and symbols, from following the lunar phases and using herbs to interacting with the four elements of earth, air, fire and water. Many witches believe that objects in the natural world have a spirit or soul – that they're alive in their own kind of way. Crystals, trees, flowers and herbs are assigned different meanings and uses, seen as having character traits to be utilized in magick and ritual. Animals and insects are assigned meanings, too, as are various types of weather, the stars and planets, and so on. The natural world is seen as something to be respected and protected, and as humanity's great teacher. Of course, not *all* witches feel that the natural world is central to their beliefs or aesthetic. Yet it is common for witches to be concerned about environmental issues and to believe in the protection of Mother Earth.

However, it's also fair to say that many witches have a fondness for consumption. We often make use of various props, tools, ingredients and other materials for spellcraft, altar decoration, and so on. Witches do not denigrate the value of the material realm and this can mean that we appreciate objects and the way they enhance our craft. But as it's also vital to respect and care for our world, each witch must surely be willing to ask themselves how they can factor environmental responsibility into their buying choices. Will you choose to ensure that you buy ethically sourced goods, made in fair conditions by workers receiving fair pay? What about buying second-hand where possible? Do you choose to cut back on buying things for your craft? Explore these questions to see where you stand.

WRITE IT

◊ Make a list of all the ethical principles that you're currently feeling sure of on your path. Don't worry if it's not a long one! Keep adding to it as you figure things out over time.

◊ Make a list of the ethical principles you're *not* feeling so sure of and explore the reasons for your uncertainty.

◊ Why is it important to give yourself permission to let your witchy ethics evolve over time?

TRY IT

◊ Choose two ethical considerations from the list I have provided above and take a few weeks to figure out actively how you feel about them. You might want to have conversations about these issues, research them and journal about them as you delve into your thoughts.

◊ Notice the next few times you strongly agree or disagree with something that you read or talk about with someone. Take note of how you react. Do you immediately assert your agreement/disagreement? Do you take time to think about it? What kinds of emotions come up? What does this experiment tell you about how you'll explore and confirm your witchy ethics?

19

SHADOW WORK

The concept of "the shadow" in psychology was given to us by the Swiss psychologist Carl Jung. He used the term to describe the area of your psyche where all the things you don't want to identify with yourself are hidden away. Lots of the not-so-tasty stuff is trapped in there, such as forms of judgement that you have about others, ways in which you've caused harm to people over time or destructive tendencies that you're not ready to accept and change. But there's also a lot of treasure locked away in the shadow, too. I'm sure you know what it's like to compliment someone's artistic talent only to find that they reject your praise and can't seem to see any value in what they've created. That could be because their skill as an artist is inside their shadow – they've not consciously accepted that it's a part of them.

The things that exist inside your shadow are often witnessed unexpectedly. You may be confronted with them during a dream or nightmare, or stumble across them while arguing with a loved one. During an unfolding scenario, you may experience an unpleasant trigger that makes you aware of a deep fear, judgement or perceived flaw that had been hidden out of sight up until that point. Such sudden confrontations with your shadow can be jarring, but if you can appreciate such experiences as learning resources then they can act as springboards for serious self-development. You don't need to wait for these unpredictable glimpses, though. "Shadow work" is the concept of intentionally stepping into your shadow, to take a look around and find out what's hidden there before it finds you.

With all this nice 'n' nasty stuff floating around in a mysterious corner of your psyche, you may not always be in the best position to assess your own choices and motivations. This is why many people have an interest in their shadow and actively seek to reveal its contents. Once you can witness something that's been tucked away in shadow, you can integrate it. In other words, you can accept that it's a part of you. You can only nurture a talent once you recognize that you have it. In much the same way, you can only deal with a bad habit or address a toxic mindset once you admit that it exists. When we do our shadow work, we are agreeing to journey into areas of denial and obliviousness. We start shedding light on what has been in darkness, so that we can move forward in a more empowered way, armed with self-awareness.

This work can be a kind of psychospiritual cleansing for witches, helping us to ensure that we are responsible and perceptive practitioners who don't end up using our powers in destructive ways. I personally don't want to bring all kinds of baggage into my witchcraft and operate from my brokenness and pain. Shadow work helps me to conduct myself from a place of clarity and power in witchcraft, knowing that I'm holding myself accountable and working on myself in a profound way. When you practise witchcraft, you're making a lot of decisions. You choose when to do spellcraft and what to cast spells for. You choose your level of commitment, the things you want to study and the kind of witch you want to become in the future. You're opening up to high-impact ideas and experiences, and it's likely that you expect this to change your life for the better. You're also holding yourself to certain standards, like sticking to a schedule and toeing your own ethical line. All this may lead you to want a keener sense of who you are *in full* – not just the parts that feed your ego. Getting a more complete sense of your flaws, insecurities and judgements can help you ensure that you're only casting spells that you really believe in rather than acting on impulse. Shadow work could help you clock the times when you're acting out of malice or fear, giving you the opportunity to rethink your strategy.

LET'S KEEP GROWING

There are a lot of people running around in this world doing all kinds of far-out magick without once stopping to consider that they might not be in the best position to mess around with such strong stuff! If you're filled with anger, pain or unresolved issues that you've never really examined or healed from, your witchcraft journey could get a bit sketchy. You may not be in the best position to make decisions about how to direct spells or even what you want to achieve. Going after revenge by ruining an enemy's life can be destructive when you could instead focus on healing, strengthening and succeeding in your own endeavours. You may also end up misdirecting a lot of anger toward undeserving targets.

As a witch, understanding your motivations for the things you're doing is what gives your journey meaning. Sure, you could say that you're seeking witchcraft as a way to deal with your misery, uncertainty or disempowerment, but is the craft really enough to help you resolve all that – or do you need other strategies and forms of support, too? Getting involved in the craft can sometimes mean you're not confronting the issues that scare you or the problems that keep holding you back. The more you cast spells, read Tarot cards, etc, to try to get rid of deep difficulties, the more you may end up embroiled in them. The tools and practices of the craft can definitely be healing and illuminating. But they can also be an escape route for people who don't want to take personal responsibility for their issues. When you look at your shadow stuff, you're saying that you want to address anything that might need your attention, rather than using your craft to avoid it.

As for the *treasure* in your shadow? The skills, strengths and positive character traits? It's obvious that having access to these could help you level up in your craft, as well as across the board. A witch who sees what they're capable of is a true force of nature.

Is Shadow Work for You?

It may not be the right time on your life journey to drag the contents of your shadow into the light. You may feel an aversion to the idea as you're reading about it now, or maybe you *can* see yourself doing it, but not for a while. Even if you've done shadow work successfully before, you may not be well positioned for it currently, as it can obviously bring up stuff that's not altogether pleasant. If you'd like to do some shadow work but you're questioning its suitability, try using these ten questions as contemplation or journaling prompts:

1. Why are you interested in shadow work and what do you think you could gain from it?
2. How do you tend to deal with criticism from others when it comes up?
3. What does your answer to the previous question tell you about how you might deal with your shadow stuff?
4. What kinds of themes and issues do you expect to find in your shadow and why?
5. How would you deal with finding unexpected and/or shocking things in your shadow?
6. What would it be important to remember during shadow work and why?
7. Do you have a network of supporters and resources to turn to if you found your shadow work was getting too tough to handle alone?
8. What excites you about the idea of doing shadow work?
9. How do you think shadow work could enhance your witchcraft?
10. What do you imagine could be the worst-case and best-case results from a period of shadow work at the current time?

A basic shadow work technique

The idea with shadow work is that what you resist tends to persist – what you suppress will predominate. If you've got an *awareness* of your shadow stuff, you can ensure it doesn't end up taking over and causing issues for you.

1 If you've decided that you'd like to do some shadow work, you can begin by identifying the uncomfortable spots by assessing different areas of your life. What makes your hairs stand up a bit? What makes you feel scared, unsure, angry or kind of embarrassed? Here's a list to work through – check for the parts that you'd rather skip over:

- Friendships
- Family life
- Love relationships
- Parenthood
- Self-image
- Home and location
- Work and career
- Studies
- Spirituality
- Sex and intimacy
- Attraction and desire
- Creative pursuits
- Finances
- Mental health
- Physical health
- Gender identity
- Racial identity
- Sexual identity
- Injustice and oppression
- Political beliefs
- Community
- Future plans
- Past experiences
- Social media
- Organization
- Time management
- Boundaries and limitations
- Communication
- Conflict
- Competition and envy
- Obligations and responsibilities
- Failures and setbacks
- Independence
- Death and loss

2 Ask yourself if it's possible to journal about those weird bits and dig down into what you may have been avoiding, downplaying or deeply fearing. Try writing some statements to accompany your shadow findings. The statements should express what you've realized about the things that really bother you. For instance:

- *I've never really felt connected to my siblings and it bothers me that they seem closer to each other than me.*

- *I'm always scared that I won't have enough money for basic things, even when I logically know I'm covered.*
- *I keep avoiding the changes I want to make to my diet and lifestyle.*

3 Read back over your statements. You may realize that you don't have answers for why you feel the things you've written down – and that's OK. In your shadow work, you can first acknowledge that the statements are reflective of tough truths about how you're feeling and where your life is.

4 You can then explore the statements by reading them aloud to yourself (in front of a mirror, if you feel called to do so) and journaling about how they make you feel and why. You can work with each statement by answering the following questions about it:

- What does the issue/feeling remind you of and why?
- What are the possible roots of the issue/feeling?
- What could be positive/uplifting about this shadow finding?
- What is a good first step in dealing with it?
- What is the hardest thing about taking that first step?
- If you don't take that first step, what will happen and how will your life look?
- What do you need to keep in mind when this shadow comes up in you?
- What are at least three examples of this shadow coming up in life situations?
- What could you have done differently in each of those three situations?
- How could healing be brought to this piece of your shadow?
- How might you need to make amends for times when this shadow has caused trouble?

LET'S KEEP GROWING

- At the end of these questions, what have you realized?
- At the end of these questions, what still needs to be figured out or explored?

5 You may want to repeat the journaling process on one or more separate occasions – new layers are pulled back when we revisit something a few times.

One thing I've shadow worked a lot over the course of time is my relationship with anger. I haven't always had a healthy relationship with this emotion, and I've caused suffering for myself and others as a result. I still struggle with it, but knowing that it's an issue helps me to correct my course much faster when I go off track. I have mindset measures in place to ensure that I don't turn into an exploding volcano over the tiniest thing. I've witnessed the patterns in the way I display and process anger, so I know when I might be unduly angry or when my anger response can become problematic. I've also learned to "get behind my anger" to witness what else is there, rather than assuming that I'm simply enraged by something. I've learned that anger can mask other emotions that may be more difficult for me to deal with, such as sorrow or loneliness. I make a commitment to sit with those feelings, too. And you can do exactly the same with your hot-button issues in shadow work.

You may also want to try these other ways of exploring your shadow stuff:

- Make a piece of art to express an aspect of your shadow.
- Perform a ritual to symbolize your discovery of a piece of your shadow, or progress that you have made in integrating it.
- Speak with a loved one or online community engaged in similar shadow work.
- Work with a counsellor or therapist on your shadow stuff.

SHADOW WORK

- Keep a notebook specifically to record your shadow work findings.
- Speak your honest truth into a mirror while holding your gaze (either literally or in your imagination), to help to make the shadow discoveries more real for you.
- Create a servitor to help you feel strong, protected and focused during shadow work.
- Map out your shadowscape as you learn about it, by making a diagram or creating lists of shadow content, or using sticky notes to make a shadow "tree" on your wall.
- Use Tarot/oracle cards, runes or another divination tool to guide you to aspects of your shadow that you may be overlooking. For instance, I like to draw a Tarot card to answer the question, "What am I missing in my shadow work?", or "What would a good shadow work topic be for today?"
- Decide on a series of experiments to test how far you've come in integrating a piece of your shadow. For instance, if you've been dealing with shadows around over-giving and toxic generosity, you may want to challenge yourself to go out with some friends and avoid offering to pay for things. See how well you do and write about what helped and hindered you during the experiment.
- Learn about different techniques that people use for shadow work and try them out to discover what really works for you.

Here are some important things to remember about shadow work:

You can stop at any time

If you start to find shadow work too overwhelming or you don't see any positive pay-off after a few sessions, you may decide that it's not a healthy activity for you. If this happens, it's not a failure in any way. Stepping away from shadow work may offer you the time and energy to explore other self-development avenues that do have benefits for you, and you may feel called to return to working on shadow stuff at another time.

LET'S KEEP GROWING

You can choose the techniques that work for you

Trying different things will bring you to an understanding of what works for you. There's no one-size-fits-all approach. For example, some people favour the use of ritual in their shadow work, while others never use it. Some are heavy on the journaling, while others prefer to explore their shadowscape in counselling sessions or through making art. Find your fit.

Keep your positive intentions in mind

Exploring your shadow is not about finding material to beat yourself over the head with, poptart. Don't bully yourself with the information you find while doing this work. Remember that you're doing your shadow work so you can have a better relationship with yourself and others, and be a responsible, self-aware rebel witch. It's not so you can find ammunition for the bitchy 'n' brutal playground bully inside you. Be kind to yourself. Don't talk to yourself in a way you categorically wouldn't use on others. Absolutely no one is perfect. Everyone has their shit to sort out. Your shadow stuff is nothing to be ashamed of or hate yourself for.

You're no less of a witch if you don't do shadow work

Frankly, aside from the fact that it may not be a healthy time in your life to do this kind of work, it may also simply not appeal to you. Not everyone wants to spend extended time swimming around in the dark side of the psyche. Maybe you're struggling to see the benefits of doing shadow work and you feel you'd rather trust yourself just to deal with issues as they come up through life. That's fine and it doesn't say anything about your witchy capabilities or commitment.

You may not be someone who feels they can do shadow work alone

You may want to do this work as part of a discussion group, or with one other person or with a professional. Solo work of this nature can lead a person to feel particularly weighed down by their findings, and the voice of their inner bully may come up strongly. Some people also find it boring or confusing to do alone and stray from the aim of it, wondering where it's all going. Working alongside someone else can create a sense of structure and an opportunity to discuss progress and where the stubborn shadow stuff is still causing issues.

You may need to limit your shadow work

The flip-side of finding shadow work boring and confusing is that some people find it a bit too tasty and end up overindulging. I'll admit, I've been totally fascinated by my own shadowscape. Discovering things in there can be rather like walking through a museum of myself, looking at all the exhibits and coming to a sharpened understanding of my own feelings, fears and behavioural patterns. But it's better to step out of the shadow work process and reflect on what has been learned for a while before jumping back in, to ensure that you're really using and appreciating your realizations.

You can only do your shadow work

Always ensure that your explorations come back to the place of self. If a lot of your shadow working seems to centre on what someone else's problem is or why other people are wrong, you've strayed from the path. Even if you think you've got a pretty good handle on how other people need to change their behaviours and perspectives, that's *their* stuff. Whether or not they'll ever get around to that important work is up to them. Your agency lies only in *your* shadow work. So, when you're focused on someone else, gently remind yourself that you want to bring it back to self. Refocus on where *you* need to take responsibility, what *you* need to realize, how *you've* been acting out, etc.

WRITE IT

◊ What are the top three things you think you may need to explore in shadow work at this point in life and why?

◊ Unsure about whether you want to try shadow work at this point in your life? Use the list of ten questions above as journal prompts to get clarity on this.

TRY IT

◊ Choose three shadow work techniques, either from this book or from other resources or your own devising. Try out the techniques in three separate sessions, working on the same piece of shadow stuff each time. Rate the three techniques from one to ten and consider why you found them more or less useful to you.

SEEKING HELP
AND SOLVING
YOUR PROBLEMS

Listen, honey bee – it's important to know that there's no shame in witches seeking help *outside* their practice. If you're struggling with life, witchcraft can form an incredible part of the path toward healing and empowerment. But it's unlikely to be the entire solution. In fact, there's a danger of some people seeking out witchcraft as a means of escape, to avoid fully dealing with their problems, and that's just not going to get you anywhere good in the end. If you know that your reasons for witching are connected to past traumas or present problems that are really troubling you, then there's nothing wrong with calling in all the support and understanding that you can get, and not all of it is going to be found in sacred space. Rituals, spells and connections with beings provide so much empowerment and healing for many witches, and yet they still also attend therapy, use helplines, take medications or join support groups.

Try asking yourself these questions:

- How are you currently coping with life's challenges?
- What's the potential value of reaching out to someone – personally or professionally – for help with what you're going through?

- What are the key non-witchcraft techniques that you tend to use when things get tough in life?
- Which issues are getting to you a lot right now and what are the witchy *and* non-witchy actions you could take to deal with those?
- Take a look at an issue that's currently troubling you: which aspects are within your agency and which, realistically, are not? (You could research answers/techniques, ask for help or get up earlier to give yourself more time, for instance, but you're probably not going to be able to affect things like the weather, the economy or the results of an election.)
- Why is it important to focus more on what's within your agency than on what's outside it?
- What kind of role do you want witchcraft to take in your journey of self-development, problem-solving and wellness?
- What would it be unrealistic to expect from witchcraft in your journey of self-development, problem-solving and wellness?
- What's the most helpful part of your witchy practice when you're feeling particularly low or lost?

Being a witch doesn't negate your issues, and witches have shit to deal with just like everyone else. You haven't failed simply because magick didn't solve everything. Magick can be incredibly helpful, but there could be other steps you need to take along the way. Rather than avoiding those steps, you can use magick to help you take them. Cast spells to help you build the bravery and empowerment needed to seek help. Perform a ritual to symbolize your readiness for positive change. And do whatever you need to do outside your craft to seek support and utilize advice.

Be honest with yourself about what you use your practice for and how realistic you're being about the results. If you're in a lot of debt, for instance, of course you'll use spellcraft as a part of your journey toward financial freedom. But should you stop there? Or would it also be sensible to take actions such as calling a debt-management helpline, calling your creditors, making a budget and so on? Let's say you're very fearful of taking those kinds of steps. Well then, do a spell to help you release your fear so you can take decisive action. It's no use just doing a spell to get yourself out of debt if you also know that you've spent months avoiding the practical steps required to deal with it. Spells can be potent, but they are usually going to be far more effective if you direct them to where they're most needed. If you're struggling to pick up the phone to talk about your debts, do a spell to help you prepare for that task and to be strong during the phone call. This is when spellcraft is at its most useful – when we take it from "make my debt disappear" to "make me strong enough to face the issue, take the practical steps and grow as a result".

Before casting a spell, performing a ritual, doing a reading for yourself or asking a being for guidance, make sure you're using your witchcraft in the most beneficial way. Allow it to be proactive rather than avoidant. Ask yourself:

- Is this witchy act going to help me face the issue and proactively move through it?
- Is this witchy act going to be a good use of my energy and focus at this time?
- Do I feel empowered when I think about the witchy act I'm about to perform?
- Do I truly believe that the witchy act I'm about to perform will help me with my issue?
- Have I also accessed non-witchy tools and support to help me, to the best of my present ability?

If the answer to these questions is yes, then whatever you're cooking up in your cauldron is going to be high-powered – do it! It could be a ritual to welcome mindset shifts or release worry. Maybe it's a spell to help you see what you're not seeing about the situation. It could be a request for support, strength or success from a goddess. Do it, as long as you feel it will *really* help with the issue as opposed to allowing you to *ignore* the issue for a bit longer. There's a key difference between someone who is just playing at being a witch and someone who knows that this witchcraft stuff *works* because they're actually applying it to problems and seeing those problems being solved.

LET'S KEEP GROWING

WRITE IT

◊ What are your current key issues and how have you been taking witchy and non-witchy action to deal with them?

◊ What are the most important things to remember when using your witchcraft to solve life's issues?

◊ What, if any, issues have you *already* solved using witchy resources, non-witchy resources, or a combination of both? How does it feel to know that you can celebrate those wins?

TRY IT

◊ Think of a long-standing problem that you've been avoiding. Write down a list of at least three practical steps that you know you've been putting off – steps that would lead to solving the problem. Consider how you could use witchcraft to help you take those steps. (Remember, you're going to be using the craft to help you *take* the steps, not to avoid/jump over them.)

21

TROUBLESHOOTING

Forget about striving for perfection. It's a mirage. Every time you think you're close, it will disappear and reposition itself somewhere else on the map. You're likely to end up flustered and frustrated, focusing on unrealistic expectations instead of appreciating your witchhood for what it is. There can be certain phases on the journey where learning is accelerated, practice is consistent, and everything is basically top banana on the witching front. But at other times, doubts, slumps or lack of time to practise the craft may leave you feeling like you're not worthy of the word "witch". Witchcraft is like anything else in your life – you've got to take the crunchy with the smooth.

Let's explore some of the potentially crunchy stuff here. This chapter is intended to prepare you for things that *might* occur in the future, and also to reassure you, when you have a challenging experience, that you're not alone. It's not intended to freak you out by convincing you that all this stuff is inevitable. Witches all have their own issues. Lean into the advice where it resonates and don't forget to revisit it along the way if you need to.

When things don't work or feel underwhelming

First things first – wait it out. I've done readings for myself that initially felt confusing or didn't seem to reveal anything, only to find the meaning becoming crystal clear later. I've written off spells only to witness them wildly manifesting in much fizzier ways than I'd hoped for. Some rituals have felt a bit dull in the moment, but gave rise to important reflections in the weeks afterwards. Our culture of instant gratification can harm our perception of time and value, and if something doesn't instantly make us feel sparkly, we can be too quick to write it off. Keep an open mind, keep going with your witchcraft and let things come together in good time. Perhaps you're just being impatient. While witchy impatience can be a sign of enthusiasm, it can also dull the shine of the experience.

Also bear in mind that not *everything* you do on your path should result in a massive payoff. As a rebel witch, you're an explorer and inventor, trying things out to see what sticks and what may need to be tweaked. You can choose to be just as interested in finding out what *doesn't* flick your witchy switch as you are in discovering what *does*. If you try something and the results are underwhelming, record that in your Book of Shadows and move on. Be proud of yourself for giving something a whirl, and avoid dwelling on the flat outcome. Finding the styles of spellcraft and ritual that make sense for you isn't a straightforward process, so try to be enthralled by the journey rather than wishing you'd already arrived.

Sometimes, underwhelm is the result of confusing the difference between fantasy witchcraft and the real thing, so keep that in mind, too. Any witch who's attempting to defy the laws of physics, bring about world peace or control everyone in their life like a bunch of enchanted puppets is setting themselves up for stark disappointment. I've always found that witchcraft *complements* reality rather than entirely departing from it, and reality doesn't include being able to fly or making everything perfect all the time.

Not believing in your powers or in magick

Choosing to embark on a witchy path implies that you're at least willing to *try* to believe in its validity and benefits. Perhaps you've been hearing and reading about how much it has helped others, and you've seen people who seem to be thriving through embracing their witchhood.

Try to hold on to these observations when your sense of belief feels a bit flimsy. Sometimes everyday consensus reality can be so cold, hard, grey and dreary that it's easy to feel as if magick is a faraway concept that doesn't have much to do with your life. We all feel this way sometimes – it doesn't mean you're a bad witch. Keep coming back to the reasons why you're walking the witchy path and remind yourself that if it's helped other people, it can help you, too. The more you do witchcraft yourself, the more you'll be offered proof that it works. And if your witchcraft *works*, then it's real.

If you're having a particularly dull day and you don't feel at all witchy, try switching on your "magician's mindset". This means increasing your awareness of the wonder and meaning that's all around you by finding the magick in *everything*. I often switch on my magician's mindset while on a walk. For 10 or 20 minutes, I see everything that I encounter through my five senses as a symbolic morsel for me to digest and use. A bird in the sky is immediately translated into a sign from my goddess. The colour of clothing worn by a passer-by suddenly has a rich meaning just for me. The lyrics from a song pumping out of a car window offer a message of clear guidance to help me solve a problem. When I take on magician's mindset, I'm ripping a hole in the fabric of mundanity and allowing it to fill with spiritual potency. Over time, you'll find that you can slip into magician's mindset naturally, without having to think about it much, and this will increase your belief in the witchy stuff all around and within you.

Finally, remember that witches have many different beliefs about what is happening when they cast a spell or even what magick really is. Some witches believe it's all in the mind and that magick is a self-transformational psychological tool. Other witches believe that non-physical beings help them to cast powerful spells. Lots of witches believe that magick is about drawing on their own divine power and that they are the gods of their own lives. Spend some time considering what *you* think it's all about. You can have your own unique philosophy of witchcraft and how it works in your life.

LET'S KEEP GROWING

Mystical magpie syndrome

Rebel witches are spoilt for choice. There's so much out there to discover and experiment with, and we give ourselves permission to try it all. "Like a kid in a sweetshop" doesn't even begin to cover how it feels to be a witch sizing up all the different techniques and tools on offer. Like mystical magpies, many witches find themselves picking up all kinds of shimmering things to embellish their witchy nests, from material objects like decks and books to all manner of different practices and areas of study. They then tend to become overwhelmed and lack direction, trying to fit too many things into a stuffed spiritual framework that's bursting with excitement but lacking real substance.

Let's have a look at some of the key symptoms of mystical magpie syndrome:

- You have a jam-packed spiritual schedule that's unrealistic and exhausting.
- You keep purchasing new things without consistently using what you already have.
- You often leave witchy books half-read, forget about them and start reading new ones.
- You're overwhelmed and confused by all the different practices you're excited about.
- You often change the labels you apply to yourself and/or never feel happy with how your witchcraft is going.
- You keep making strong starts with different practices, deities or areas of study but nothing lasts beyond a few weeks.
- Other witches always seem to have a more desirable/interesting practice than you.

If this all feels painfully close to home, try taking things more slowly for a while. When it comes to subjects to study, practices to incorporate, deities to worship, etc, there's such a thing as being spiritually saturated. You could give each new technique or tool a trial period during which you focus on it alone, without adding anything else, to find out how effective and meaningful it is for you. Maybe you want to work with a new deity for three months without approaching any other deities, or try out just one card deck for a month to deepen your relationship with it. At the end of the trial period, review how it's going and decide whether you want to incorporate it into your practice or not.

Instead of making purchases too frequently, keep categorized lists of the things you'd like to acquire. Let each new item sit on the list for at least a month while you decide if it's really necessary. Ask yourself if there are things you've already acquired that you could use – do you want to focus on them instead? This is about becoming more conscious of the value of objects in your craft, in place of convincing yourself that the next thing is going to be the thing to end all things! (Spoiler alert: It *never* is.)

Criticism and concern from loved ones

Looking to other people for permission to witch is never going to be a good idea. It's nice if the important people in your life are interested in your beliefs or – at the very least – accepting of them, but it's not a prerequisite for successful witchhood. In fact, if you're spending too much energy trying to convince others that your spirituality is OK by them, you might find you don't have enough energy to make it OK by *you*.

Remember that you don't need to tell anyone about your witchhood before you're ready, and you're not actually obliged to tell anyone at all. You're entitled to a private inner life that you can explore without sharing your thoughts about it. Perhaps consider if it will be helpful and at all positive to tell a specific person, or if this will only cause division and conflict. If you do decide to step out of the broom closet to a tough crowd, be prepared for that and set your expectations accordingly.

If you're anticipating concern or criticism from a partner, family member or friend about your decision to be a witch, keep the following things in mind as you go into the conversation:

- You don't need to overexplain. Keep it simple if need be, and be clear at the start about what you do want to elaborate on and what is off-limits.
- There's no need to have all the answers. If you're still unsure about an aspect of your path and someone questions you on it, you can simply say, "I don't know about that yet, it's something I'm still figuring out."
- It's not your responsibility to prove your beliefs. Are you asking the person to become a witch themselves? No. Well, then it shouldn't matter whether or not they doubt that it's possible to cast a spell. They're entitled to have doubts. What they're not entitled to do is disrespect you by verbally abusing you or disparaging your spiritual beliefs. You have the right to remind them of this during the conversation if need be.
- You're not responsible for managing the other person's feelings. A loved one may have a lot of emotions to unpack once you come out of the broom closet, including fear, anger and disappointment. It's OK for them to experience these emotions, but it's not OK for them to expect you to counsel them through it all, or to give up witchcraft just to make them feel better. They must go on their own journey to explore why they feel the way they do, and to ultimately help themselves to reach acceptance.
- No one has the right to out you to someone else. If you're coming out of the broom closet to someone in strict confidence, highlight that fact at the beginning of the conversation. Be sure the other person understands that they should *not* reveal any information to others.

Resisting change

Your interest in a certain practice, deity or area of study might wax and wane over time and that's OK. As you change on your life path, your *witchy* path may need to follow suit. Practices that used to be super-helpful may no longer call to you. A deity or ancestral spirit that used to converse with you frequently may eventually go long distance or even stop making contact entirely. You can leave the door open for something to come back, but don't let its absence stop you from putting more focus on other aspects of your practice. When you go through key life events, your instincts on what to pursue in your witchhood may shift. Experiencing grief, becoming a parent or moving to another country are obvious examples of events that may alter your sense of what your practice needs to look like. But even minor incidents, such as having a powerful dream or reading an influential book, can create a shift. Try to be excited about this when it happens rather than striving to keep everything as it's always been. I always say that I don't want to buy a ticket and get on the train only for it to stay on the platform. I want to feel that I've been somewhere. I always expected witchcraft to be an adventure – and I have not been disappointed.

One thing I've learned from mentoring rebel witches over time is that many have a tendency to feel guilty for dropping practices or moving away from relationships with beings. But you can't expect your interests and practices as a witch to be static throughout your entire life. Prepare for natural evolution. You will eventually be able to look back over your path and see all of the different colourful phases you travelled through. Some witches have more phases than others. Rebel witches tend to have lots. It's all part of the wonder. Don't fight it.

Inspiration versus imitation

An abundance of social media platforms makes it easier than ever to overdose on witchy content, leaving your brain drenched in all kinds of ideas and aesthetics. Can it be inspiring? Undoubtedly. Does it get overwhelming? Sometimes definitely. There's nothing wrong with being interested in hearing other witches addressing hot topics or seeing how they set up their altar spaces. But you might want to consider how you feel after imbibing that kind of content. Do you come away with a gnawing sense that your own practice or collection of witchy tools is lacking? Do you find that hearing other witches talk about their ideas makes you doubt or criticize your own? That's not a tasty place to be, sugar plum. It's OK to realize that too much witchy content can be unhealthy.

LET'S KEEP GROWING

Remember to follow *your* witchy bliss. If something that you see, hear or read has a strong influence on you and makes you feel excited, sit with it for a while and consider *why* you're intrigued. Does the tool, practice or being that's caught your eye actually gel with your current aims? Does it fit in with your beliefs? Don't be tempted to stick something into your practice just because it's trending or because it seems to be working for a witch that you admire on social media. Scrutinize your enthusiasm a bit before claiming a belief or adopting an aesthetic. Make sure it's something you want to try because you're really feeling it, rather than because it seems like a train that lots of witches are hopping on. Who cares where other witches are hopping? You do you.

Spiritual slumps

I don't know a single witch who continually maintains the same amount of commitment and activity in their practice, no matter what's going on in their lives. It's normal to find you feel super-inclined toward your practice at some times, and less so at other times. The key advice here is *do not sweat it*. Let it flow, let it wax and wane, let it do what it needs to do. Most witches tend to find their spiritual practice slumps when there's something else taking up their time and energy, such as a big work project, an illness or a significant life change. And isn't that reasonable? You might find it disappointing that your spiritual practice has decreased, but do you really need to shit-talk yourself for it or worry about it every day? Is there any benefit in convincing yourself that you *need* to practise your spirituality with *absolute* consistency and *no* flexibility? It's often better to acknowledge the slump in a non-judgemental way and assume that your practice will, in time, return to its previous level or evolve to where it needs to be.

You may experience a spiritual slump because you're not taking your path seriously and you keep putting it to the bottom of your priority list. This might be because you don't feel it's supported by loved ones or by the culture around you, which can be tough. But don't forget how much it helps you to be a practising witch. If something gives you joy and strength, try to acknowledge that and make some space for it.

Remember that you can practise witchcraft in your own mind. You don't need to wait until you're in an environment where the craft is supported and you can have an altar and talk freely about your practice. You can practise *now*, inside yourself. Try it.

Maybe your spiritual slump comes from a general lack of discipline. If you know you can struggle to stay the course with things, it's good to practise self-discipline by deciding on a regular spiritual activity and trying to keep it up. But keep your plan manageable. If you decide you're going to spend an hour or more on your witchcraft each day, you may be setting yourself up for failure because that aim is unrealistic for most people.

WRITE IT

◊ Take a look at the issues discussed above and choose one you've already encountered. Write down the advice you'd give to a witch who's encountering this problem now. How could you help/guide them? What worked for you?

TRY IT

◊ Whereabouts do you need to do some troubleshooting now in your practice? Detect an issue that you're having and consciously try to improve it for two to four weeks, checking in with your progress regularly.

◊ Find resources by other witches offering advice and support in areas that are problematic for you. What do you notice about the solutions other witches advise? Which ones are most helpful?

LET'S KEEP GROWING

22

CONNECTING WITH OTHERS

Many rebel witches have a strong instinct to work solo. I suppose this seems like an obvious choice because when you cast spells and perform rituals with others, you design the events *together*, compromising and exchanging ideas to agree on a shared vision. Rebels like to do things their own way entirely, and this can make the idea of joining any kind of coven unappealing. There's nothing wrong with simply being a solo practitioner. In fact, you don't even need to talk about your path with anyone.

But there's also a lot to be said for practising alongside other witches. If you already have friends who are also on a witchy journey and fancy getting together for spooky shenanigans, then that's great. If not, you might be able to find a group you vibe with in your local area by searching online. Or you could form a cyber coven, working long-distance with a group of witches from around the world – you could get together via online video chats to celebrate the Sabbats and other events. If this sounds appealing, maybe you could put the feelers out on social media to find people who are in an existing group or would like to join one, for either physical or digital get-togethers.

You can seek to perform rituals and cast spells with other witches if you want to, forming a coven with them. But you don't have to. You might just want to discuss each other's practices, enjoying chatting about craft stuff with people who get it and don't judge you for it. Decide what you really want and what benefits you're looking for in finding a community.

You get to choose your level of involvement with your community. You might want to attend workshops at the local witchy store, exchange messages with other witches on social media or start your own channel or podcast to share your thoughts and feelings with a wider audience. Your witchy social life could be big, bold and immersive. Equally, maybe you just want to join some online groups so you can find out what others think about the topics you're interested in, preferring not to get involved in discussions yourself. It's entirely up to you.

If you're looking to join or start a coven involving regular meetings or workings, you'll need to feel fairly certain that you're ready for that commitment. Are you able to sign up to their schedule? Will you have time to do the prep work before meetings/workings? What about compromising to achieve a shared vision – are you willing to do that?

Being involved in a wider witchy community can be inspiring and beneficial, but there can be downsides too. Check in regularly with your experience of being part of a community and make sure you feel largely positive about it. If occurrences in the community are making you feel overlooked, demeaned, paranoid, insecure or scared, you have the right to deescalate your relationship with members of the community or with the community as a whole.

If you're pursuing a sense of community so that you can learn from others, that's great. But it's wise to ensure that you're not leaning too heavily on a more long-standing witch and expecting them to provide you with an in-depth education. Avoid picking someone's brain too regularly, unless you've both agreed they're happy to mentor you. Use free resources, apply yourself to study and form your own opinions where possible.

When it comes to community, you sometimes have to kiss a few frogs before you find your prince. If you joined a coven, discussion group or witchy book club and it wasn't the right fit after all, leave with decorum. If there's a need to say goodbye formally, you can thank the other community members for the experience and try to leave on a good note. Appreciate what you did learn, but don't hold yourself to continuing within a community structure that doesn't feel right.

WRITE IT

◊ Describe your ideal witchy community situation. Is it online, offline or both? Is it a big group or small? Is there a sense of leadership or hierarchy? What does the community work on together? Try to be as detailed as possible. After writing the description, write about how you feel about the exercise and what it taught you about your own perspective on witchcraft community.

TRY IT

◊ Research stories that witches have told about their experiences in covens and other types of witchy community. Look for the good, the bad and the ugly. Get a sense of the incredible achievements of witchcraft groups working together. But don't overlook the uncomfortable, unpleasant and scandalous aspects of witchcraft groups, too.

◊ Dip your toe into a new online witchcraft community, if you feel comfortable to do so. Involve yourself in a conversation or debate. See how this makes you feel. What do you learn from this experience?

GO FORTH AND REBEL!

Well, chickpea, it's been amazing to spend this time with you. I greatly appreciate being given the opportunity to share some thoughts and I hope it's thrown some glitter over the proceedings. I wanted this book to act as a fizzy little permission slip - nothing more, nothing less. I'm not the most academic of witches and certainly not the longest in the tooth. But considering all the rules there are to follow in this reality and all the duties there are to carry out, what I do have is a deep instinct that your witchhood should be as wild and rogue as you want it to be. No one signs off on this delicious lunacy except you, honey. Be sovereign to yourself. Put your signature on it. At the end of your life, know that you did it your way and that you have no regrets about that.

FURTHER READING

There are so many worthwhile reading resources out there to nurture and inspire rebel witches. This list is a taster to point you in some useful directions.

Beginner Witchcraft

Consider these titles if you're new to the craft and in need of friendly guidance to help you take the first steps:

Tonya A. Brown, *The Door the Witchcraft: A New Witch's Guide to History, Traditions and Modern-Day Spells*, Althea press, 2019

Juliet Diaz, *Witchery: Embrace the Witch Within*, Hay House UK, 2019

Sakura Fox, *Wishcraft: A Complete Beginner's Guide to Magickal Manifesting for the Modern Witch*, Hay House UK, 2020

Deborah Lipp, *Magical Power for Beginners: How to Raise and Send Energy for Spells that Work*, Llewellyn Publications, 2017

History Lessons

Although I didn't intend for *Rebel Witch* to include anything on the history of witchcraft, I would never discount the value of accessing resources to deepen your understanding of it. Here are some books I've found useful:

Christopher Dell, *The Occult, Witchcraft and Magic: An Illustrated History*, Thames & Hudson, 2016

Malcolm Gaskill, *Witchfinders: A Seventeenth-century English Tragedy*, John Murray, 2006

Ronald Hutton, *The Triumph of the Moon: A History of Modern Pagan Witchcraft*, Oxford University Press, 2001

Ronald Hutton, *The Witch: A History of Fear, from Ancient Times to the Present*, Yale University Press, 2018

Marilynne K. Roach, *Six Women of Salem: The Untold Story of the Accused and Their Accusers in the Salem Witch Trials*, Da Capo Press, 2013

Chaos Magick

There's no doubt that chaos magick has been a huge influence for me as a witch. The ideas and techniques in these books were beyond helpful:

Adam Blackthorne, *The Master Works of Chaos Magick: Practical Techniques for Directing Your Reality*, CreateSpace Independent Publishing Platform, 2016

Peter J. Carroll, *Liber Null and Psychonaut: An Introduction to Chaos Magic*, Weiser Books, 1987

Jan Fries, *Visual Magick: A Manual of Freestyle Shamanism*, Mandrake, 2000

Phil Hine, *Condensed Chaos: An Introduction to Chaos Magic*, The Original Falcon Press, 2010

Phil Hine, *Prime Chaos: Adventures in Chaos Magic*, The Original Falcon Press, 2017

Andrieh Vitimus, *Hands-on Chaos Magic: Reality Manipulation Through the Ovayki Current*, Llewellyn Publications, 2009

Contemporary Witchcraft

Inspiring accounts and advice from modern witches doing it their way:

Phyllis Currott, *Witch Crafting: A Spiritual Guide to Making Magic*, Harmony, 2002

Jason Louv, *Generation Hex: New Voices from Outside Reality*, Disinformation Company, 2005

Victoria Maxwell, *Witch, Please: Empowerment and Enlightenment for the Modern Mystic*, HarperCollins, 2020

Arin Murphy-Hiscock, *The Witch's Book of Self-Care: Magical Ways to Pamper, Soothe, and Care for Your Body and Spirit*, Adams Media, 2019

Sophie L. Robinson, *Wellness Magick: A Modern Day Spiritual Guide for Crafting a Solid Foundation to Your Everyday Wellbeing*, That Guy's House, 2020

Kristen J. Sollee, *Witches, Sluts, Feminists: Conjuring the Sex Positive*, ThreeL Media, 2017

Katie West, *Becoming Dangerous: Witchy Femmes, Queer Conjurers, and Magical Rebels*, Weiser Books, 2019

Tarot

As I'm a professional cardslinger, this list wouldn't be complete without a few Tarot books. If you want to start learning or deepening your understanding, here are some suggestions:

Liz Dean, *The Ultimate Guide to Tarot: A Beginner's Guide to the Cards, Spreads, and Revealing the Mystery of the Tarot*, Fair Winds Press, 2015

Sallie Nichols, *Tarot and the Archetypal Journey: The Jungian Path from Darkness to Light*, Weiser Books, 2019

Arthur Rosengarten, *Tarot and Psychology: Spectrums of Possibility*, Paragon House, 2011

Benebell Wen, *Holistic Tarot: An Integrative Approach to Using Tarot for Personal Growth*, North Atlantic Books, 2015

Shadow Work

Here are some useful titles if you want to delve deeper into this riveting aspect of your own psyche:

Deepak Chopra, Marianne Williamson and Debbie Ford, *The Shadow Effect: Illuminating the Hidden Power of Your True Self*, HarperOne, 2011

Debbie Ford, *Dark Side of the Light Chasers: Reclaiming your Power, Creativity, Brilliance, and Dreams*, Hodder Paperbacks, 2001

Robert A. Johnson, *Owning Your Own Shadow: Understanding the Dark Side of the Psyche*, Bravo, 1994

Connie Zweig and Steve Wolf, *Romancing the Shadow: A Guide to Soul Work for a Vital, Authentic Life*, Ballantine Books, 1999

INDEX

WATKINS
Sharing Wisdom Since 1893

The story of Watkins began in 1893, when scholar of esotericism John Watkins founded our bookshop, inspired by the lament of his friend and teacher Madame Blavatsky that there was nowhere in London to buy books on mysticism, occultism or metaphysics. That moment marked the birth of Watkins, soon to become the publisher of many of the leading lights of spiritual literature, including Carl Jung, Rudolf Steiner, Alice Bailey and Chögyam Trungpa.

Today, the passion at Watkins Publishing for vigorous questioning is still resolute. Our stimulating and groundbreaking list ranges from ancient traditions and complementary medicine to the latest ideas about personal development, holistic wellbeing and consciousness exploration. We remain at the cutting edge, committed to publishing books that change lives.

DISCOVER MORE AT:
www.watkinspublishing.com

Read our blog

Watch and listen to
our authors in action

Sign up to
our mailing list

We celebrate conscious, passionate, wise and happy living.
Be part of that community by visiting

 /watkinspublishing   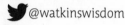 @watkinswisdom

 /watkinsbooks    @watkinswisdom